A History of the

Milton Cemetery

Anthony M. Sammarco

America Through Time

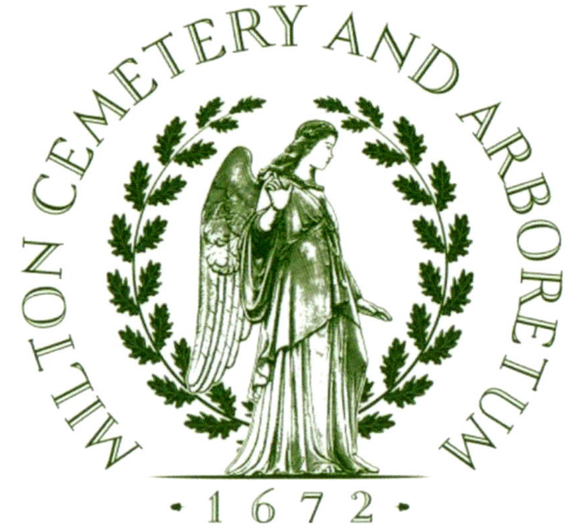

America Through Time®
An imprint of Sutton Publishing inc
www.through-time.com

First published 2025
Copyright © Anthony M. Sammarco 2025

ISBN 978-1-63499-515-3

Typeset in 10pt on 13pt Sabon
Printed and bound in England

ACKNOWLEDGMENTS

I wish to thank Edith Clifford for her research and notes for the inclusion of Milton Cemetery on the National Register of Historic Places. Her forms have important information and were of great help in my research. I also would like to thank Peter Bryant Kingman for his wonderful contemporary photographs of the Milton Cemetery, and Linda Mason Pirie for her invaluable research and interest in Milton history, as she provided many unknown and important details that have greatly contributed to this book.

I wish to extend my sincere thanks and deep appreciation to: The Copeland Foundation, Martha Verdone, John Tobin, Joyce Tobin, Mary Gormley, George Moran, Raymond Pelissier, Richard Wells, Jr.; the trustees of the Milton Cemetery: James Coyne, Joseph Reardon, Stephen Pender, Jed Dolan, Terence Driscoll, chair; Lisa Ahern, superintendent of Milton Cemetery; and Meg Toyias. I would also like to especially thank Therese Desmond who was superintendent of Milton Cemetery for three decades.

I would also like to thank the following for their support and assistance: Archives of American Art Smithsonian Institution, Marisa Bourgoin; Joyce George Bacardi; Karen Bacardi; Boston College, John J. Burns Library; Boston Public Library, the Norman B. Leventhal Map Center Collection; Boston University Libraries, Ryan Hendrickson and Jane Parr; Judge Paul Buchanan; Wendy Burden; Cesidio "Joe" Cedrone; John David Corey and Miguel Rosales; Marcia Bonaccorso Corey; The Country Club, Fred Waterman; Jimmy Coyne; Edith Cunningham Crocker; Cunningham Foundation, Jini Connors; Ulysses Grant Dietz; Douglas County Historical Society, Omaha, Natalie Kammerer; Dennis "Mike" Doyle; Association of Engineering Societies; Mary Ann English; Frederic and Elizabeth Shaw Eustis; Frances Pierce Field; Forbes House Museum, Heidi Z. Vaughan; Nancy Newcomb Frates; Hagley Digital Archives; Harvard Art Museums/Fogg Museum, Katie Kujala; Harvard University Archives, Pusey Library; Historic New England, Lorna Condon; Henry Lyttelton Alexander Hood, 8th Viscount Hood; Charlotte Dumaresq Hunt; Iolani Palace, Hawaii, Zita Cup Choy; George Kalchev, Fonthill Media; Phyllis Forbes Kerr; Mary Eliza Kimball; Darcy Kuronen; Lysa Leland; Library of American Landscape History, LALH, Robin Karson and Sarah Allaback; Robert Mcauliffe; Kathy McHale; Paul McVinney; Massachusetts Historical Society; Massachusetts Institute of Technology Libraries, Department of Distinctive Collections, Allison Schmitt; Massachusetts State House Art Commission,

Susan Greendyke Lachevre; Medford Historical Society, John Anderson and Susan Gerould; Metropolitan Museum of Art; Vincent J. Miles; Milton Academy Archives, Laura Pearle; Milton Historical Society, Dan Haacker; Milton Public Library, William L Adamczyk and Jean Hlady; Eileen Buchanan Moncreif; Steven Morris; James G Mullen Jr.; Museum of Fine Arts, Boston; New York Public Library; Orleans Camera; Adele Eells Pierce; Mary Pierce Pillsbury; Polly Pillsbury; Lilian M.C. Randall; Rosalie Channing Rivers; James Adams Roberts; Nancy Pattison Roberts; L. Perry Russell; Kara Thompson Russo; Schlesinger Library, Harvard Radcliffe Institute, Diana Carey; Ron Scully; Ann Sheffield; Kena Longabaugh Smith; Eileen Sturner; Carolyn Stetson; Ann Hollidge Strout; Roger Sullivan; Alan Sutton, Fonthill Media; Jamie Sutton; Swarthmore College Peace Collection, Victoria Russo; Robin Tagliaferri; Judith Tankard; Tavern Club, Nancy Maull; Tufts University Digital Library; Archives and Special Collections, University of Massachusetts, Sammarco Collection; Hannah Dray Vokey; Edward Bowditch Watson; Tony Will; Marion White Woodbridge.
I would like to especially thank Sheila Monks for kindly proofreading this book.

Photographs, unless otherwise credited, are from the collection of the Milton Historical Society.

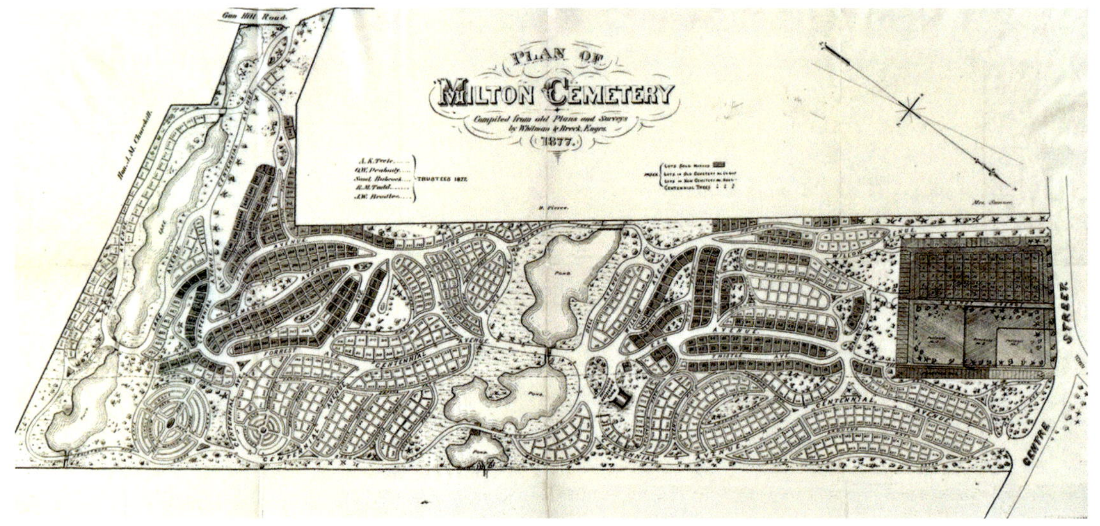

The "Plan of Milton Cemetery Compiled from old Plans and Surveys by Whitman & Breck, Engrs." was drawn in 1877. (*Milton Cemetery Archives*)

CONTENTS

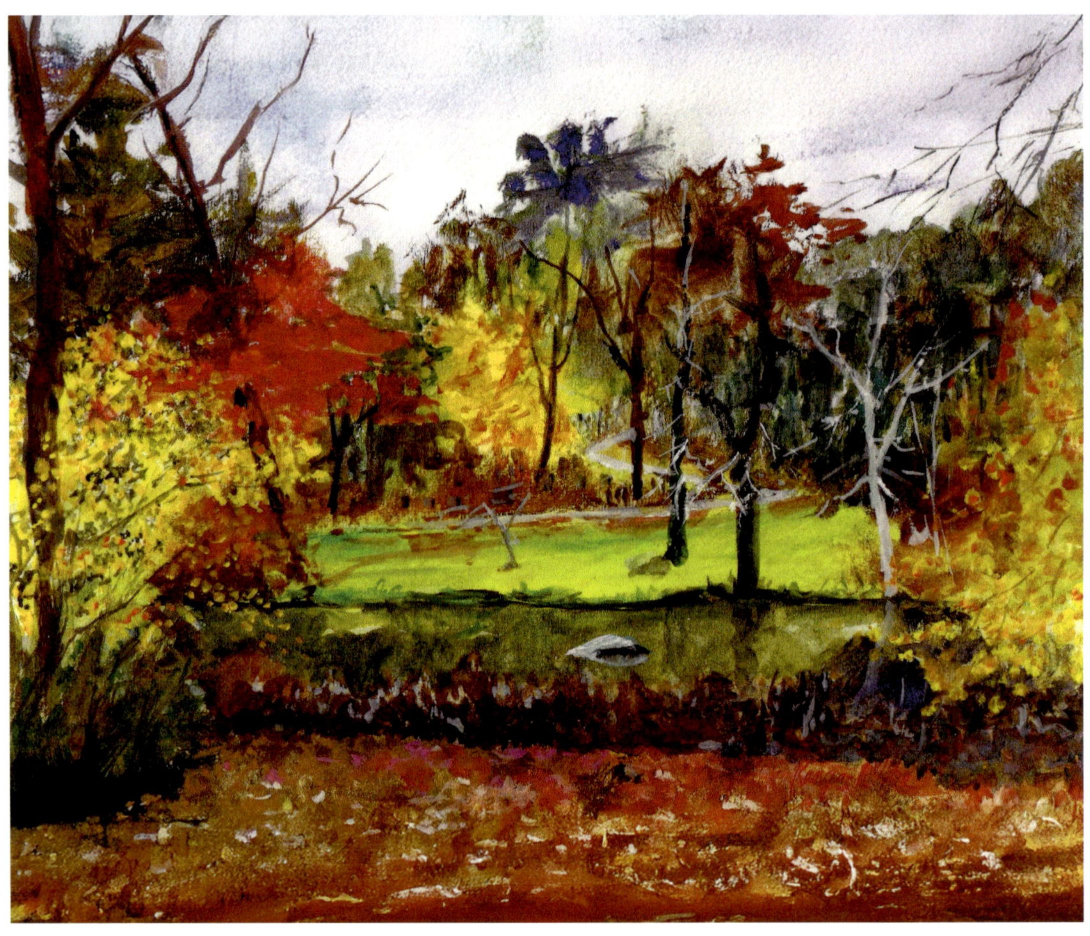

Thanksgiving Morning is a watercolor of the Milton Cemetery Duck Pond by Dennis "Mike" Doyle, fondly known as *Ranger Mike* of the National Parks Service. Painted in 2019, the vivid colors show the bucolic quality of the duck pond with a rock rising above the surface of the water, surrounded by hardwood, conifer, and deciduous trees. The pond, which is in the central part of the cemetery, was an important feature of the rural landscape movement of the nineteenth century as an attractive and bucolic setting. (*Author's collection*)

$\mathscr{I}$ NTRODUCTION

Milton Cemetery was established in 1672 as the place of burial for those who had once lived in the town. Known as the Field of Reedman, it was just six rods by seven rods, or roughly 99 feet by 115 feet, and is today known as the Olde Burying Grounds. The cemetery has been the only place of burial in Milton Massachusetts over the last three and a half centuries and continues as an active place of burial with 102 contiguous acres which are characterized by curvilinear avenues and paths set in a rolling terrain of hills, dells, and valleys with mature trees, shrubs, gardens, and a duck pond.

Milton, Massachusetts was once a part of Dorchester, which was settled in 1630 by Puritans from England seeking religious freedom. Dorchester was once a sprawling town that included South Boston, Squantum, Milton, Canton, Stoughton, Sharon, Foxboro, Wrentham, and Raynham, all of which would become independent towns. Before the settlement of Massachusetts Bay Colony by the Puritans, the land had been inhabited by the Neponset tribe of the Massachusett, an Algonquian people, who referred to the area that would become Milton as "Unquatiquisset," meaning "Lower Falls," the place where the rapids of the Neponset River meet Massachusetts Bay. Milton, just south of the Neponset River, would be founded in 1640 and become an independent town in 1662, remaining farmland, with small industries along the Neponset River, well into the nineteenth century.

It is not known if those living in Milton used the burial ground at Cemetery Corners in Dorchester (now the Old North Burying Ground in Upham's Corner and laid out in 1634), or an unknown area in Milton. Albert K. Teele said that "the supposition is that the inhabitants [of Milton] had been using the field of Reedman for this purpose, and thus were led to fix upon this place as the common burial-ground." The first reference to a burying ground being established was in the *Milton Town Records* (Volume 1, Page 1) and states:

The 24 Feby. 1672. Robert Reedman was allowed to be payedd out of the towne Rate tene shillings to pay for forty rods of Land for the Burying Place appraised and staked out by Anthony Gulliver, William Blake, Robert Badcock, Robert Reedman being present and consenting thereto—and was agreed betwixed the Towne and Robert Reedman that the towne should fence out this forty rods of land, with a sufficient stone wall, withing two years, from Robert Reedman's Land.

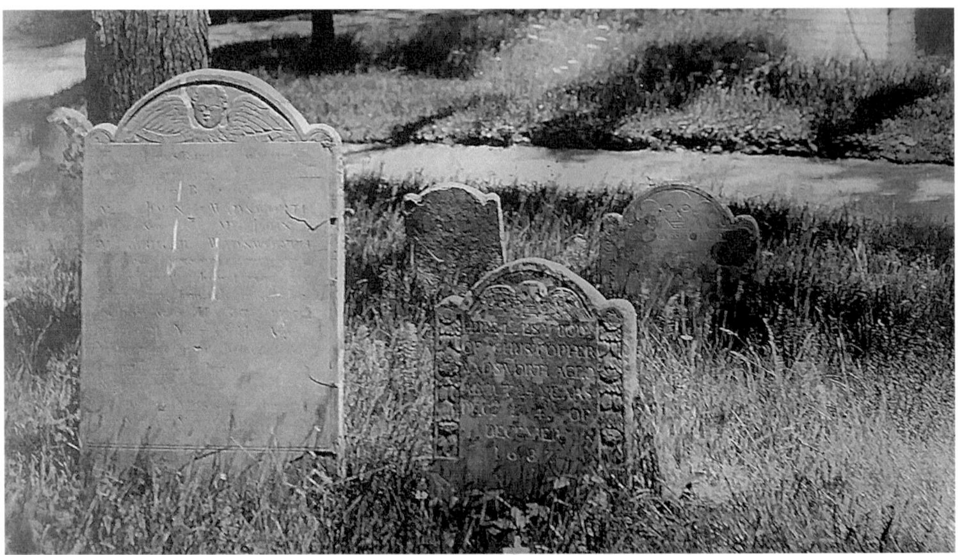

The winged skull headstone of Christopher Wadsworth (1663–1687) is the oldest extant marker at Milton Cemetery. He was the son of Captain Samuel Wadsworth who was said to be a "resolute, stout-hearted soldier" of King Philip's War. His brother was Rev. Benjamin Wadsworth who served as president of Harvard College from 1725–1736. (*Courtesy Milton Public Library*)

Here Lyes ye Body of Christopher Wadsworth, aged about 24 years, dec'd 4th of December 1687.

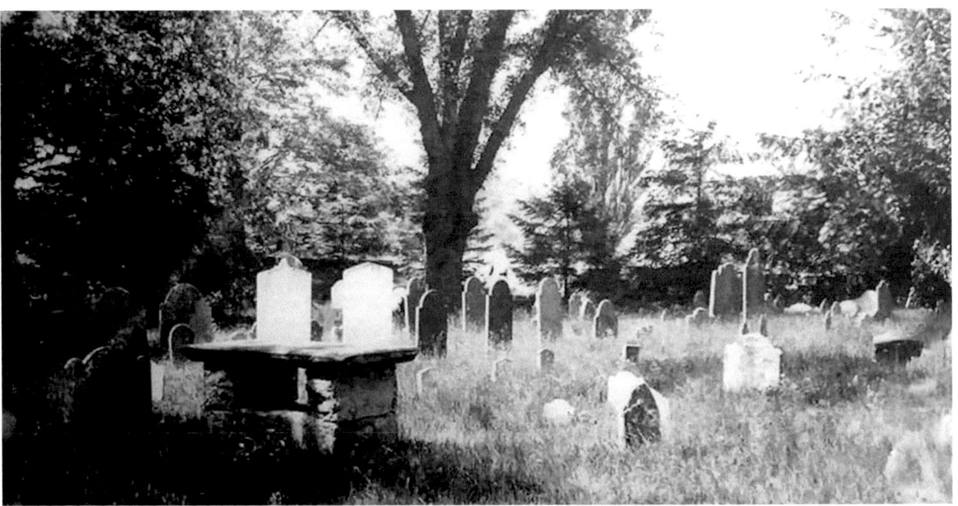

Theodora Oxenbridge Thacher (1659–1697) was the daughter of Rev. John Oxenbridge, pastor of the First Church in Boston, and the wife of Rev. Peter Thacher (1651–1727), the first pastor of the Church at Milton. The table stone marker was made of Connecticut brownstone, set on supports resting on a large base. (*Courtesy Milton Public Library*)

Mrs. Theodora Thacher ye daughter of ye Rev'd Mr John Oxenbridge Past'r of ye First Church in Boston & Wife of Mr. Peter Thacher aged 38 years 3 months 25 days was Translated from Earth to Heaven Nov'r ye 18th 1697.

Little is known of Robert Reedman, or Redman as Rev. Albert Teele referred to him in *The History of Milton, Mass.* His house was on what is now Churchill's Lane and the land acquired for the burying place, laid out only a decade after the town was incorporated, was located on Centre Street across from his house lot. The burying ground was sufficient in size for the town, as in 1662 there were said to be only 250 residents, according to Edward Pierce Hamilton. However, as time passed, the need for additional space became necessary and land was acquired by the town by both purchase and gift. In 1699, a committee was appointed to secure additional land to increase the "burying place fild." The Reedman Lot was enlarged in 1729 with the Ministerial Tomb Lot, the Foye Lot in 1760, the How-Vose Lot in 1794, and the Amory Lot in 1837. Not surprisingly, there is a wonderful overlay of funereal motifs on the headstones representing well over three centuries in this area.

The Ministerial Tomb, marked by a rectangular white marble memorial, was an impressive mound tomb that was built at the request of the Thacher Family for the burial of Reverend Peter Thacher (1651–1729) who had served as minister at the Milton Meeting House and was known as the "noted theologian and Congregational clergyman." This was to become the ministerial tomb and used well into the mid-nineteenth century. In 1719, three tombs at the edge of the burying ground, built by the Fenno, Miller, and Billings Families with permission granted by the town selectmen. The extant slate headstones represent a wide range of funereal iconography that primarily represent skull and crossbones, but it is important to note that the "Puritans were adamantly against attributing human form to spiritual beings such as God, angels, or spirits. The death's head, a non-religious symbol was the first imagery employed in gravestone carving." However, one must also realize that not every grave was marked and that undoubtedly some headstones have been lost over the years. Puritans, in adherence to the second biblical commandment, "Thou shalt not make unto thee any graven image," the Puritans avoided the worship of ancestors through stone images.

The 1687 headstone of Christopher Wadsworth is the oldest extant headstone in the cemetery and the evolving iconography from the seventeenth century of grim death's heads that extolled the Puritan virtues and beliefs, to the eighteenth-century winged angels that offered hope and solace in death as the realistic imagery evoked human decay into the skulls and crossbones. Some families in Milton had headstones carved by noted stonecutters whose skill and knowledge, including the selection of slate from outcroppings, shaping them, preparing their faces, and carving the reliefs was to become an early form of folk art. Among those whose carvings are known in the Milton Cemetery are James Foster II, one of a family of noted stone carvers from Dorchester, which often depicted a human face with wings which were less morbid than the skulls, possibly reflecting an abiding faith in the afterlife. William Mumford of Boston was one of the more skilled carvers and his carvings have distinctive side borders often containing fruits and gourds.

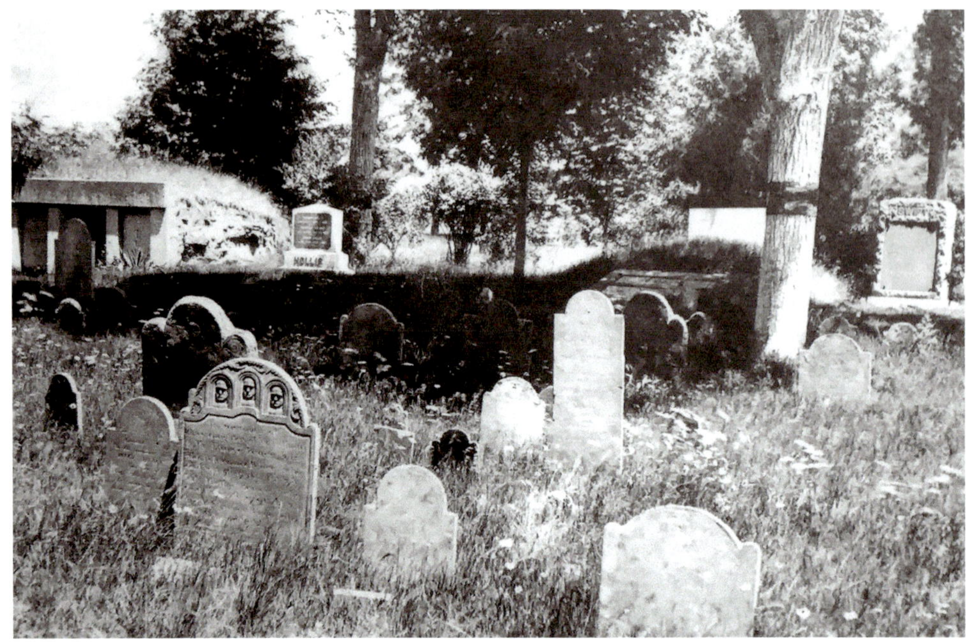

A late nineteenth-century photograph of Milton Cemetery, looking east, had seventeenth- and eighteenth-century slate headstones in the foreground with the wall tomb of E. C. Tucker and A. Crehore on the far left and the granite monument of Edwin Macomber. There are slate headstones interspersed with granite monuments, creating an overlay of three centuries of funereal designs. In the foreground is the headstone of the daughters of William and Eunice Pierce, Miss Deliverance Pierce, died 1792; Miss Martha Pierce, died 1791; and Miss Eunice Pierce, died 1788. (*Courtesy Milton Public Library*)
Lovers and Friends, Oh God! By thy resistless frown,
The gloomy vale have trod, And to the grave gone down.

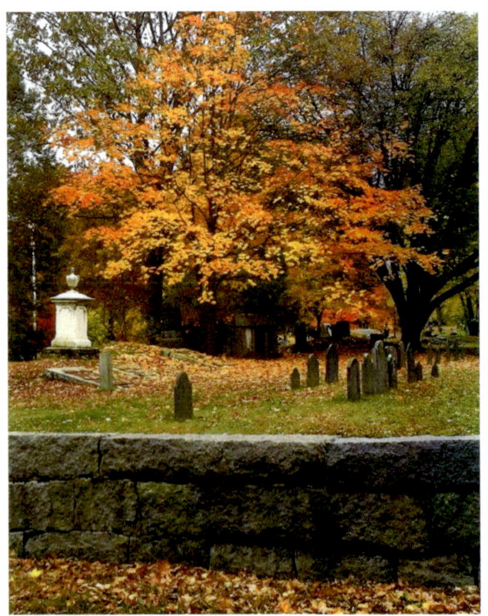

The Olde Burying Grounds, seen from Centre Street, are vivid with color during the autumn. The massive granite blocks create an impressive wall built in 1859 that runs along the street and in the distance can be seen eighteenth-century slate headstones. On the left is the neoclassical white marble urn surmounted memorial to Daniel Vose (1741–1807) who was chairman of the Milton Committee of Correspondence. It was in his house at Milton Village that the Suffolk Resolves were signed and taken by Paul Revere and delivered to the Continental Congress in Philadelphia, where it was ratified as the "Declaration of Rights" on October 14, 1774. (*Photograph by Peter B. Kingman*)

Henry Christian Geyer, a German immigrant who arrived in Boston in the 1750s, was a skilled carver of gravestones often with smiling skulls sporting deep gouged eye sockets and deep gouged nose holes as well as winged heads. The simplicity and straightforwardness of the early stones were the personification of the Puritan ideology that the "ethic envisions work as a symptom of salvation, and a person with poor work ethic is sinful. The Puritan work ethic is an intensification of the normal valuation of a person's work ethic." These symbols reflect the Puritan values which were in practice from 1672 to the early eighteenth century. The winged skull symbol pertains to life and death, and possibly might suggest the briefness of life and the power of death, something that would impact everyone regardless of their position in life.

The headstone of Joseph Fenno from 1767 is poignant in its prose:

> *In the cold mansions of the silent tomb,*
> *How still the solitude, how deep the gloom,*
> *Here sleeps the dust unconscious, close confined,*
> *But far, far distant dwells the immortal mind.*

It is known that there was often little embellishment of Puritan burying places. In 1689 Enoch Badcock was instructed by the Selectmen of Milton to "procure bords and nails, and to fence in our burying place, he using the posts already brought to place for the same use … [and] to pay him … in Oates at twelve pence pr bushill, Indian corn at tow Shillings pr bushill, ry if any, at tow Shillings pr bushill." Granted, payment in grain for his work sustained Badcock's family, but in 1761, it was "Voted That Mr. Josiah How improve our Burying Place for the space of five years, by feeding of sheep to subdue the bushes and briers that are therein." In 1697 at Milton Town Meeting, it was voted to build on "two sides of the burying place fenced with good sufficient Stone wall of four feet and a half hye, and to fence the other two sides for the present with the ould posts and board already there."

Throughout the first half of the eighteenth century, there were various attempts to enlarge the burying place, but the owners of the abutting lands refused to sell their land to the town. Over the next two centuries, however, the expansion was to include seven tracts of land.

The First Enlargement was the gift in 1760 of Madam Elizabeth Foye, the widow of William Foye who served as treasurer of the Province of Massachusetts Bay, and her daughters, Elizabeth Foye and Mary Foye Cooper. This gift was of a half-acre and six rods of land for the price of one shilling.

The Second Enlargement was the purchase of land from the heirs of Deacon How of half an acre and 22½ rods, and from Colonel Joseph Vose of 17½ rods of land.

The Third Enlargement was the gift in 1837 of Francis Amory, Esq. "in consideration of one dollar and divers other good causes" of one and a quarter acre of land. Armory donated to the town in 1837 the sum of $500.00, the income of which was to be annually expended for the care of the graveyard.

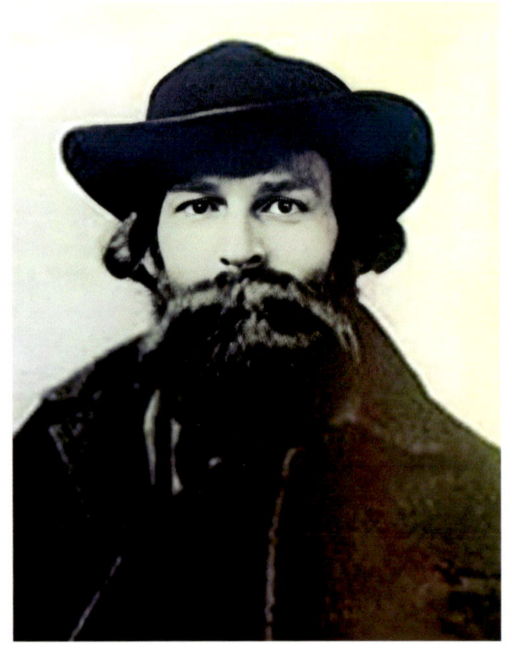

Robert Morris Copeland (1830–1874) graduated from Harvard College. In 1854, he began a partnership "in landscape and ornamental gardening" with Horace Cleveland and their projects included the Sleepy Hollow Cemetery in Concord, Massachusetts, and the Oak Grove Cemetery in Gloucester, Massachusetts. He was commissioned first lieutenant with the 2nd Massachusetts Infantry during the Civil War and became quartermaster of the regiment. Known chiefly for his cemetery plans, he would work on the grounds of the Milton Cemetery, creating a rural, or arboretum cemetery, so popular in the mid-nineteenth century. (*Courtesy of Allen Mitchum, Jr.*)

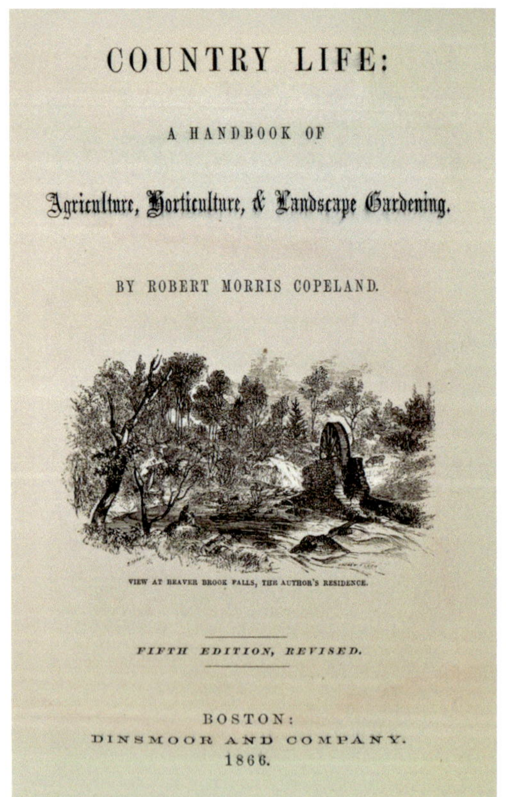

Country Life: A Handbook of Agriculture, Horticulture and Landscape Gardening was written by Robert Morris Copeland and published in 1866. In this book, Copeland offered "practical and aesthetic advice to rural citizens and suggested that a managed rural landscape offered everything that might expand the mind and ennoble the soul." This book was to become a virtual bible of scientific farming and landscape gardening, as it incorporated the latest agricultural practices with new engineering methods. He and his partner, Cleveland, laid out the curvilinear pathways and landscape design at the Milton Cemetery, the methods and design of which are espoused in this book. (*Author's collection*)

The Fourth Enlargement was the purchase by the town from Charles Breck and Thomas Hollis, Jr., in 1854 of 18 acres and 116 rods of land for the sum of $1,804.00.

The Fifth Enlargement was land acquired from Joseph McKean Churchill of a lot of land near Gun Hill Street for $125.00. As Churchill said, it was "from love and affection for my native town and the inhabitants thereof, in order to furnish a convenient access to the New Cemetery lately purchased and laid out by said town."

The Sixth Enlargement was the gift of land in 1870 from Charles Marshall Spring Churchill to straighten the boundaries with a stone wall with fond "regard to his native town and in consideration for one dollar."

The Seventh Enlargement was the purchase in 1874 of 12 acres of land.

In the 1840s, Daniel L. Gibbons and Elijah Vose "undertook the improvement of the [cemetery] grounds, which had long suffered from neglect," and by soliciting funds from family and friends would plant elm, evergreen, and other trees "along the south and west sides of the cemetery, outside the grounds." Also, by the mid-nineteenth century, Milton Cemetery was to see further improvements under the direction of the Rev. Francis Cunningham, minister of the Third Religious Society in the Lower Mills and husband of Mary Abbot Forbes Cunningham, as it was under his guidance that "the work of improving and embellishing the Cemetery grounds received an impulse which has never been lost." In the mid-nineteenth century, the two-century-old cemetery would be reinterpreted from a town burying ground into a rural cemetery by a movement that swept across the United States. Père Lachaise in Paris had been the prototype of a new aspect of burial and would greatly influence cemeteries being laid out with impressive drives and a tree canopy. Before the widespread development of public parks, the rural cemetery would change the perspective towards death and the burying of the dead, while also providing a place for the public to enjoy outdoor recreation amidst art and sculpture, as well as green space. In essence, this movement would replace the dreary, dark burial grounds with the reimagined cemeteries evolving into an almost celebration of life, and the beauty of nature surrounding it. Milton Cemetery, which had evolved since 1672, was to see newly acquired land laid out by noted landscape architects who introduced this new vision using naturalism to show how the nineteenth-century Romanticism influenced the Rural Cemetery Movement. Horace W. S. Cleveland, Robert M. Copeland, and Ernest W. Bowditch were three influential landscape architects who would design new places of burial while retaining natural features such as ponds, streams, and mature stands of trees, while laying out winding roads and paths that followed the natural contours of the land, as well as the planting of native trees and plants. These "arboretum" cemeteries were not only popular but suited the Victorians perception of death and burial, with family lots large enough to allow the burial of several generations, while also ensuring a place that was to conform with the rural aesthetic.

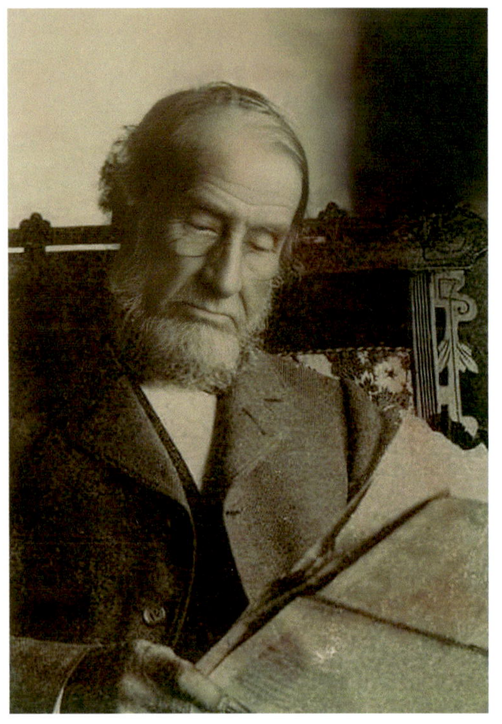

Horace William Shaler Cleveland (1814–1900) was a noted landscape architect whose designs enhanced the Milton Cemetery. His approach to landscape design was novel and he would experiment as a scientific farmer, considering both practical and aesthetic issues of landscape design, and would publish articles about pomological techniques in journals such as Andrew Jackson Downing's *The Horticulturist*. He was the author of *Landscape Architecture as Applied to the Wants of the West*. It was said that Cleveland was "a preservationist by nature, respecting the natural landscape features around him and shunning unnecessary decoration." (*Courtesy LALH*)

Copeland and Cleveland published *Landscape and Ornamental Gardening* which was a business outline of their philosophy as to how the landscape could be enhanced by working with nature. They were highly regarded and were to submit a design for New York City's Central Park which lost out to Frederick Law Olmsted. Their vision of rural cemeteries would help to shape public and private landscapes of the nineteenth century not only in New England but in the expanding American West. (*Courtesy of LALH, William H. Tishler Collection*)

In 1854, Horace William Shaler Cleveland and Robert Morris Cleveland began as pioneer American landscape architects in landscape architectural design and received the commission to design Sleepy Hollow Cemetery in Concord, using their interpretation in the rural cemetery aesthetics. They eschewed the more traditional burial grounds on the seventeenth and eighteenth centuries for the more "tasteful disposition of trees and shrubs, with graceful adaption of the roads and paths to the natural contours of the ground." In this regard, Milton Cemetery was to see new winding avenues, with side paths, laid out by Breck & Breck, a prominent Milton survey firm of Charles Breck and his son, Charles E. C. Breck. The cemetery was embellished with a prominent entrance on Center Street that had impressive iron gates, the rebuilding of the stone wall along Centre Street, the planting of elms along the new avenues as well as a Receiving Tomb that was necessary to hold future burials during the winter months. According to Rev. Albert K. Teele, the work of improving and embellishing the Milton Cemetery grounds began in earnest in 1865 under the guidance of the Rev. Francis Cunningham.

The cemetery grew apace of the need for more land, and in 1874, a 12-acre tract of land was purchased from Charles M. S. Churchill and was laid out by Whitman and Breck, a survey firm that complimented the earlier design by Copeland and Cleveland. Their "Plan of Milton Cemetery Compiled from old Plans and Surveys by Whitman & Breck, Engrs." was drawn in 1877 and appears as a fold out map in Teele's *The History of Milton*. It shows lots in the Old Cemetery, lots in the New Cemetery, and lots sold by 1877 as well as the Centennial Elm Trees, named for the centennial of the United States, which were planted along the avenues.

In 1877, in the center of an ornamental plot of single and charitable graves encircled by Circle Avenue was a gently elevated area in the center of the cemetery. In the center of the circle on a marble plinth is an angel of white marble which was carved in Italy, and donated by Henry Purkitt Kidder, co-founder of the investment house Kidder Peabody & Company. With a sense that land could be at a premium, the trustees voted "that hereafter no space be left between lots, but that paths be left at suitable intervals in the discretion of the superintendent." In 1883, the Duck Pond was created by dredging the land and was laid out and became a bucolic focal point encircled by various trees. The nineteenth-century landscape, which has remained intact to this day, was the result of three very capable and well-known landscape architects and is today an admired feature of the grounds.

Horace William Shaler Cleveland

Pioneer American landscape architect whose vision reaching beyond this time lives on in the rivers, parks, and parkways of the Twin Cities. They are his true monument.
Horace William Shaler Cleveland (1814–1900) was a noted landscape architect whose designs greatly enhanced the Milton Cemetery. Born and educated at an innovative school in Lancaster, Massachusetts, his lack of a traditional education was to see the emphasis on landscape study and observation. He went to Cuba in the 1820s where he learned about mulching techniques on the coffee plantations and healthful effects of the climate. Moving to Burlington, New Jersey, he experimented for a few years as a scientific farmer, considering both practical and aesthetic issues of landscape design

and would publish articles about pomological techniques in journals such as Andrew Jackson Downing's *The Horticulturist.*

In 1854, Cleveland moved to Massachusetts and began a practice in landscape and ornamental gardening with Robert Morris Copeland. Cleveland wrote that to be successful in the landscape architecture field, one must "Look forward a century, to the time when the city has a population of a million and think what will be their wants." Their first important commission was the design of Sleepy Hollow Cemetery in Concord, Massachusetts, for which Copeland and Cleveland were employed by Ralph Waldo Emerson and the members of the Concord Cemetery Committee. At this time, their fundamental beliefs in the communicative and restorative powers of nature on the landscape fully emerged. Cleveland and Copeland designed the site to be sensitive to the existing landscape, and as a park connected to various public open spaces in the Concord community.

It was in the 1850s that Cleveland and Copeland began work at the Milton Cemetery, and in 1854, they announced that they were in the business of Landscape and Ornamental Design and offered to "furnish plans for the laying out and improvement of Cemeteries." They would later work on cemeteries in Gloucester, Waltham, Melrose, and Bridgewater in Massachusetts, Yarmouth, Nova Scotia, and Bangor, Maine.

Their ideas about the connection of public space informed their suggestions for a Boston Park system a year later. In 1856, as the Back Bay was being infilled, Cleveland and Copeland recommended that Commonwealth Avenue connect the center of Boston, the Common and Public Garden, to public spaces on the city's periphery. It was interesting to note that Cleveland and Copeland had submitted a plan for the creation of Central Park in New York. Cleveland said that "The tract of land selected for the Central Park comprises such an extensive area and such variety of surface as to afford opportunity for the construction of a work which shall surpass everything of its kind in the world." Both he and Frederick Law Olmsted, who won the commission, suggested "broad lawns, undulating surfaces, clothed with the rich verdure, dotted here and there with graceful trees and bounded by projecting capes and islands of wood."

Cleveland and Copeland dissolved their partnership sometime before the Civil War. Moving in 1869 to Chicago, Illinois, Cleveland worked with business leaders to "guide the advance of civilization by planning." During the 1870s, he worked on Chicago's Drexell Boulevard, the South Parks, and Graceland Cemetery and published *Landscape Architecture as Applied to the Wants of the West with an Essay on Forest Planting on the Great Plains*, one of the first books to define and develop the scope of the new profession of landscape architecture.

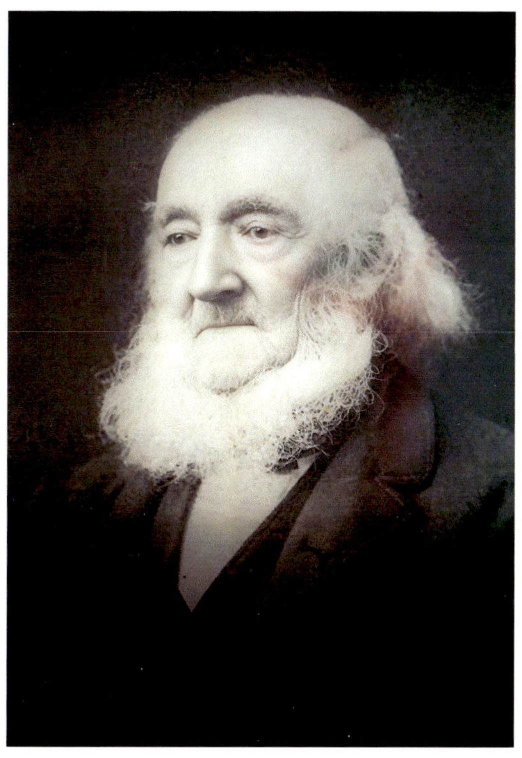

Charles Breck (1798–1893), known as "Honest Charles," was a farmer, wool puller, and tanner before taking up a career as surveyor with his son as Breck & Breck. In 1837, he was first elected to the Milton Board of Selectmen, beginning five decades of public service in various town offices, including serving as the town's treasurer for thirty-four years. He was also active as an officer of the First Congregational Church of Milton and as director and agent for the Quincy Mutual Fire Insurance Company. From 1849–1888, he kept a daily record of temperatures outside his home at sunrise and 1:00 p.m. These weather observations were published in *Annals of the Astronomical Observatory of Harvard College.*

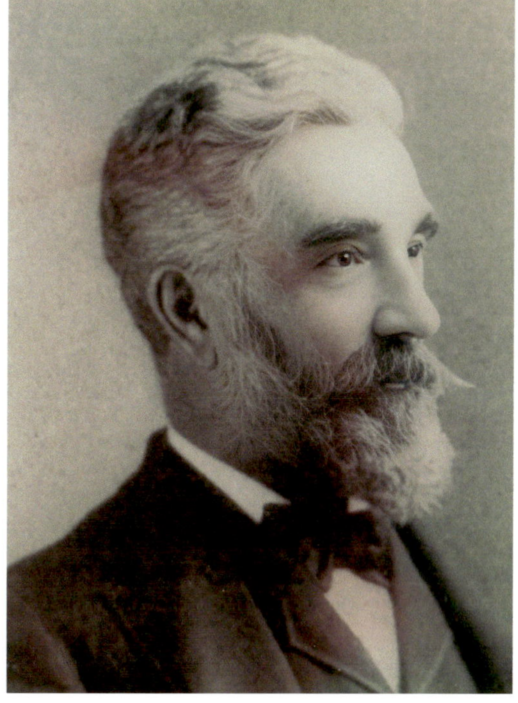

Charles Edward Cushing Breck (1834–1899) was a well-known surveyor who worked with his father, Charles Breck, in the firm of Breck & Breck. He served in the Civil War in Company B of the 45th Regiment as a private and was later promoted to sergeant. In 1870, he joined Herbert Taber Whitman in their surveying firm of Whitman & Breck. The firm engaged in the laying out of Wollaston in Quincy and the towns of Winthrop and Revere. The firm also laid out the Narrow Gage Railroad from East Boston to Lynn, and the Fore River shipbuilding plant in Quincy.

Robert Morris Copeland

He helped establish the foundations for city planning and integrated park systems.
Robert Morris Copeland (1830–1874) was born and raised in Roxbury, Massachusetts, and attended Harvard College. He began his career as a scientific farmer at Beaver Brook Falls in Belmont, Massachusetts, which was renowned for its woodlands, wetlands, and a cascading waterfall. His house was set amongst the impressive Waverly Oaks, a stand of twenty-two white oak trees which would be defended from destruction in the late nineteenth century by landscape architect Charles Eliot.

In 1854, Copeland began a partnership "in landscape and ornamental gardening" with Horace Cleveland. Copeland's projects with the firm included Sleepy Hollow Cemetery in Concord, Massachusetts, the Samuel Colt estate in Hartford, Connecticut, and the Oak Grove Cemetery in Gloucester, Massachusetts, as well as the Milton Cemetery. In 1856, Copeland joined forces with Henry Wadsworth Longfellow to write a pamphlet entitled *A Few Words on the Central Park* which outlined the failed landscape design submission to the Central Park design competition in 1857. In 1859, Copeland published *Country Life: A Handbook of Agriculture Horticulture and Landscape Gardening* in which he offered "practical and aesthetic advice to rural citizens and suggested that a managed rural landscape offered everything that might expand the mind and ennoble the soul." In that book, he criticized the Boston Common, calling it "mutilated due to missed aesthetic opportunities and discussing the choices he would have made to improve it." In 1859, Copeland agreed to design the layout for Mount Feke Cemetery in Waltham in exchange for $325.00 and his choice of a lot within the cemetery where he was eventually buried.

After parting ways with Cleveland, Copeland served in the Civil War and was commissioned a first lieutenant with the 2nd Massachusetts Infantry and became quartermaster of the regiment. In 1861, he was recruited by former Governor of Massachusetts Major General Nathaniel Banks and was appointed his aide-de-camp, after which Copeland was appointed his assistant adjutant general with the rank of major. He lobbied and helped establish the 54th Massachusetts Regiment, the black brigade later depicted in the famous movie *Glory*. However, Copeland overstepped himself and was critical of President Lincoln and was subsequently dismissed from service for "having violated an important trust committed to him while serving on the staff of the general commanding the Department of the Shenandoah." His reputation was ruined, but in 1870, he received a telegram by order of President Ulysses Grant, stating that his dismissal was "hereby revoked and his resignation is accepted to take effect Aug. 8, 1862."

Copeland went on to develop a well-regarded landscape architecture practice in New England. His projects included a master plan for the Frederick Billings estate in Woodstock, Vermont, and the design of the Oaks Bluffs community at Martha's Vineyard. In the 1870s, he engaged in forestry study and in scientific farming experiments consistent with many of the ideas presented in his book *Country Life*. Highly respected, he was one of the Incorporators of the Massachusetts Institute of Technology when it was founded in 1861.

In 1872, Copeland published *The Most Beautiful City in America: Essay and Plan for the Improvement of the City of Boston*, in which he championed the idea of a

Boston parks system. He continued to refine his design philosophy and worked to position himself to design a system of parks for Boston until his unexpected death in 1874, without realizing his dream of a unified parks system for the city. After his death, his apprentice, Ernest W. Bowditch, continued to promote Copeland's concept for a connected park system in Boston. According to his obituary "Copeland had done much in the way of laying out and ornamenting private grounds, but his ambition was for work on a grander scale."

Whitman and Breck

Civil engineers and surveyors.
Howard Taber Whitman was born and raised in Pembroke, Massachusetts, and started his career as an apprentice to Luther Briggs, Jr., one of the noted architects, land surveyors and civil engineers of nineteenth-century Boston. Briggs lived in Port Norfolk in Dorchester and as Dorchester Town engineer, laid out that neighborhood as well as Harrison Square, now referred to as Clam Point. In 1868, Briggs laid out Cedar Grove Cemetery in Dorchester and Whitman worked as an apprentice on the project.

Charles E. C. Breck was the son of Charles Breck, a farmer, wool puller, and tanner before taking up a career as surveyor, insurance agent, and town treasurer of Milton, Massachusetts. Charles E. C. Breck was educated in the Milton public schools and took a supplementary course at Milton Academy. In 1855, he took up land surveying with his father and their company was known as Breck & Breck. In 1862, he enlisted in Company B of the 45th Massachusetts Regiment and served until the end of the war. After his return, he farmed at his home *The Butternuts* on Brush Hill for a few years and, in 1870, formed a partnership with Herbert T. Whitman as civil engineers and surveyors.

Whitman & Breck opened an office in 1870 in the Joy Building on Washington Street in Boston. This partnership as civil engineers and surveyors was fortuitous as Boston was to see tremendous growth in the mid-nineteenth century. The business was successful and Whitman and Breck received the commission to survey the Town of Revere, Massachusetts, with Whitman taking the uplands and Breck taking the marshes. This led to land company layout work under the sponsorship of George F. Pinkham at Arlington Heights, Wollaston, and Chelsea, Massachusetts. They were commissioned to survey the new town of Hyde Park which was created in 1868 from sections of Dorchester, Dedham, and Milton. Alpheus Perley Blake, a man of indomitable character and a tireless worker, was the promoter of the Milton neighborhood of Fairmount through the Twenty Associates and is regarded as the Father of Hyde Park. The land, from Brush Hill Road to the Neponset River, was developed in the 1840s and would be ceded by Milton to the new town of Hyde Park. In the 1870s, Blake was promoting the development of Revere, Massachusetts, and Whitman & Breck were employed by him to lay out and supervise the building of the Boston, Revere Beach & Lynn Railroad, known as the Narrow Guage Railroad, as well as the areas of Orient Heights, Beachmont, Revere Beach, Point of Pines, and Winthrop, which would have passenger stations built for commuters. Whitman & Breck were also involved in building the railroad tunnel in Jeffries Point, East Boston, the Saugus River Bridge, the Great Ocean Pier near Beachmont, and the Fore River shipbuilding plant.

In 1877, the town of Milton commissioned Whitman & Breck to survey and make a detailed plan of Milton Cemetery, which was "compiled from old plans and surveys," one of which was a now lost plan of the cemetery drawn by Edmund J. Baker in 1841. This plan shows the Old Burying Ground from Centre Street with lots numbered from 1 to 600 clearly marked, as well as lots in the New Cemetery starting at 601; they designed the entrance from Gun Hill Street in 1877. Whitman & Breck went on to make a street plan of Brookline, but there was also work in East Boston, Winthrop, Revere, Dorchester, Hyde Park, Milton, and Quincy around Boston, and at Boothbay, Magnolia, and Martha's Vineyard.

In 1886, Whitman and Edward Breck's partnership ended, with Whitman buying out Breck, who was said to have retired unwillingly although he continued as a surveyor and civil engineer. Whitman, who was said to be one of the most prominent surveyors and engineers in Massachusetts, joined with Channing Howard to form Whitman & Channing.

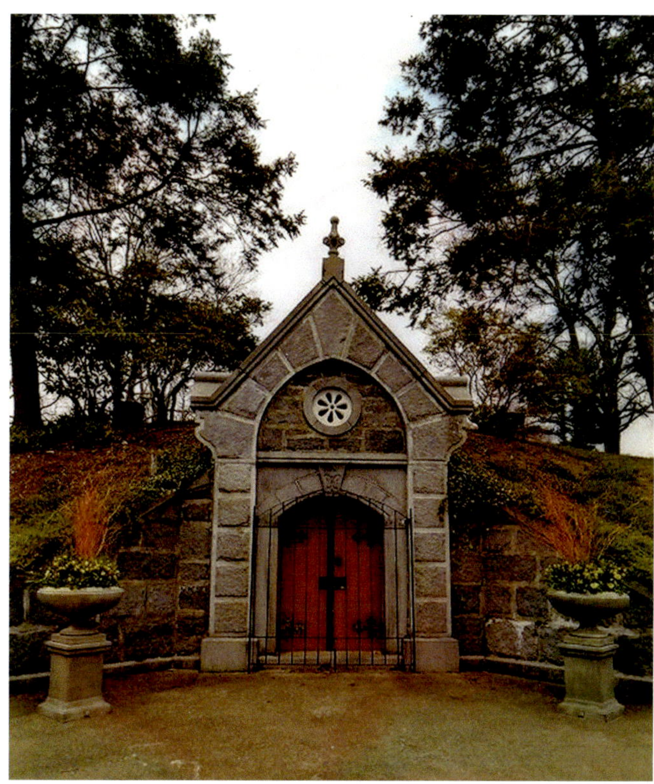

The Receiving Tomb, once an important building during the winter months when internments could not be made, was built in 1879 by the O. T. Rogers & Company, a well-known granite company in West Quincy. The Gothic-like structure was built of large rough hammered granite blocks with a curved retaining wall that extends to either side. Today, technological advancements in excavation have rendered the receiving tomb obsolete, but it still is an attractive feature to the cemetery. (*Photograph by Peter B. Kingman*)

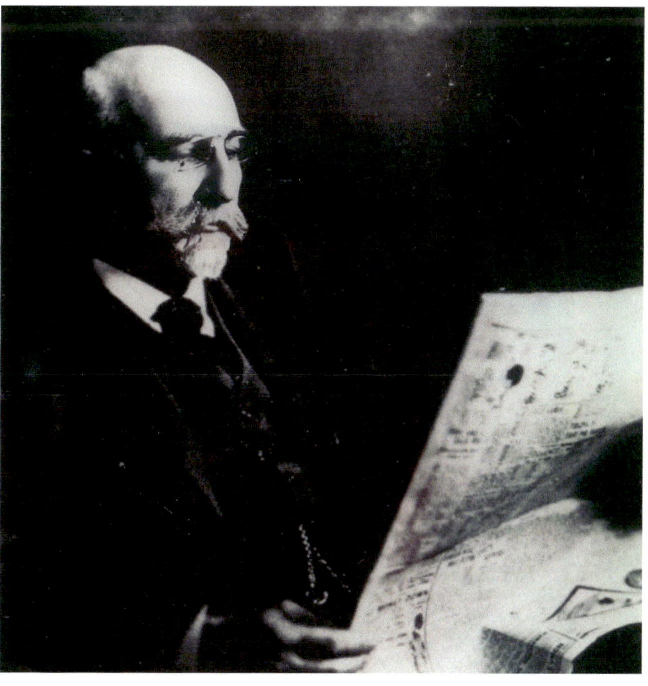

Ernest W. Bowditch (1850–1918) graduated from the Massachusetts Institute of Technology in 1869. In 1870, he became a member of the United States Expedition to the Isthmus of Darien, later known as the Panama Canal, working as a topographer and geologist while surveying for the future canal. He later worked for Shedd and Sawyer, civil engineers, and went on to establish his own practice in Boston. He worked as a landscape architect and sanitary engineer for many years and was highly respected in the field. He was one of the more well-known landscape architects of the early twentieth century and oversaw the laying out of Milton Cemetery. (*Author's collection*)

Ernest W. Bowditch

Landscape gardener and civil engineer.

William Ernestus Bowditch (1850–1918) was born in Brookline, Massachusetts, and educated in the Brookline public schools. In 1865, Bowditch (who inverted his first and middle names and was to become known as Ernest William) studied at the Massachusetts Institute of Technology but left in 1869 without a degree and went to Nebraska, where he had a construction job with the Chicago Burlington & Quincy Railroad.

In 1870, he returned to Boston and was appointed assistant mineralogist with the Darien Expedition, a canal survey expedition to the Isthmus of Panama. He worked in conjunction with architectural and engineering firms, as well as using his family connections to obtain independent commissions. His career is marked by associations with prominent Boston and New York architects, landscape architects and architectural firms such as Robert Morris Copeland, McKim, Mead & Bigelow, Frederick Law Olmsted, Bruce Price, Peabody & Stearns, H. H. Richardson, and Shedd & Sawyer.

Bowditch was employed at Shedd & Sawyer, civil engineers, in 1870 and his first job for the firm was general maintenance of the grounds of Mount Auburn Cemetery in Cambridge, where he laid out driveways, paths, stone bounds for corners, curbing, and gardens, which proved to be a great impact on Bowditch's evolving design ideas. In the mid-1870s, he opened his own office which he shared with his brother, James Higginson Bowditch, who worked as a landscape gardener. He often did survey work for Robert Morris Copeland, Frederick Law Olmsted, and John Charles Olmsted, as a surveyor or draftsman. He also collaborated with H. H. Richardson on several projects, notably working as structural engineer for Boston's Trinity Church.

Bowditch not only laid out parts of Walnut Hills Cemetery in Brookline but was to lay out a large tract of land donated by Oliver White Peabody, a co-founder of Kidder Peabody & Company, to the Milton Cemetery. He was a talented and gifted designer, both creatively and technically, as well as an adept manager of project construction. He was involved in municipal surveys for sewer and water supply design in many eastern communities, as well as structural engineering, land surveying, cemetery design, subdivision layout, and landscape design at summer resorts of the wealthy, especially Newport, Rhode Island. While much of Bowditch's residential design was carried out in a picturesque style, his designs for the estates of the wealthy often utilized a more formal layout. His own estate was *Eastover*, designed by McKim, Mead, and White which was built on Milton Hill. He also designed the Eustis Estate, with a stone mansion designed by William Ralph Emerson, which was one of his early projects. Interestingly, his daughter Elizabeth Swann Bowditch married Augustus Hemenway Eustis.

Bowditch had become well known and his commissions were often for wealthy clients. He was to design Newport, Rhode Island estates, among them The Breakers and Chateau-sur-Mer. In fact, he provided landscape designs for several subdivisions such as Tuxedo Park in New York, Newton Terraces in Waban, and Allston Park in Allston, Massachusetts as well as Shoreby Hill in Jamestown, Rhode Island. The suburban Cleveland communities of Clifton Park and Euclid Heights were also designed by him.

There were many improvements at the Milton Cemetery in the last decade of the nineteenth century, with new iron signs bearing the name of the avenue or path marked upon them, but in 1879, a Receiving Tomb was built to replace the hearse house which had been built in 1837. The new tomb was designed by O. T. Rogers & Company, a well-known granite company in West Quincy. The founder, Octavius T. Rogers (1802–1859), was a prominent granite dealer who not only had his own quarry and cutting sheds in Quincy but had worked on the Bunker Hill Monument, Harvard College Library, the Boston Merchant's Exchange Building, and the granite gateway to Mount Auburn Cemetery. The Receiving Tomb is built of large rough hammered granite blocks with a curved retaining wall that extends to either side, set into the side of a gently rising hill. The tomb has a small round window set in the gable of the Gothic façade and an impressive wooden door with brass hinges embellished with a fleur-de-lis design. Important in the nineteenth and early twentieth century, it was recorded that the Receiving Tomb was "simply for the safekeeping of the remains of those who pass away, until the proper opportunity for interment arrives." Also, a new house was voted to be built for the superintendent at the corner of Centre Street and Randolph Avenue. Designed by John Atherton Tucker, a local builder, and built in 1889, this impressive Queen Anne style house adjoined a stable that would later be repurposed as the cemetery office.

The Milton Cemetery Records were unfortunately destroyed in a fire in the early 1880s, which prompted the Trustees of the Cemetery to publish in 1883 *A Catalogue of the Proprietors of Lots together with A Record of Ancient Inscriptions on all Tablets in the Cemetery Prior to and Including A.D. 1800*. The trustees at that time were Oliver White Peabody, Samuel A. Burt, Albert K. Teele, Amor L. Hollingworth, and J. Walter Bradlee, all eminent residents of Milton. However, the men employed to maintain the cemetery grounds and dig the graves were increasingly of Irish descent as Milton had seen many workers choosing the town as their place of residence, as well as for employment. In fact, it was recorded in Thomas W. Pond's 1920 Superintendent's Report that "the Catholics are taking lots much faster than formerly, and that he [Pond] may be asked to remove a number of bodies from Mt. Calvary Cemetery" in Boston to the Milton Cemetery.

The Old Burial Grounds had once been lined with early nineteenth-century wall tombs on three sides, similar to those that survive on the south or left side, and in 1886, the trustees of the cemetery sent a letter to the Proprietors of the Tombs stating that "it would be a very great improvement in the form of burial, and in the suitable and permanent identification of the remains, if these tombs were to be given up and the remains buried in the lots and properly marked. To facilitate this, the Trustees [of Milton Cemetery] offer to buy the tombs." Shortly thereafter the removal of the above ground granite tombs along the rear and right side began and the remains once in the tombs were buried in lots provided by the cemetery, and those with underground vaults were filled in with soil to grade. Some of these tombs had been abandoned by the families, and their removal allowed the cemetery to flow easily from the Olde Burying Grounds to the newly laid out areas. The granite lintels that once marked many of the family tombs above the entrance were repurposed and often used to mark the new graves, while others were discarded and reused as tree guards near the Gun Hill Road entrance with family names still clearly visible on the granite blocks. The only tomb to remain intact was that of the Baxter Family, which had been built in 1859.

A tract of 22 acres was purchased by the town in 1897 from the estate of Oliver White Peabody which substantially increased the size of the cemetery. In 1898, Ernest W. Bowditch surveyed the newly acquired land and made a "plan of avenue, paths, ornamental spaces, reserve spaces, and lots for the land lately purchased of Colonel Peabody's estate." The cemetery employees planted trees and shrubs and emulated the embellishments started in the 1850s by Cleveland and Copeland. However, even cemeteries had to move with the times and embrace change. As with any public spaces, the safety of people visiting the cemetery was paramount and there were some interesting votes taken by the trustees such as in 1893 stating that there were "notices forbidding shooting in the cemetery" and in 1897 that "lot owners be allowed to ride bicycles in the cemetery, when visiting their lots." In 1912, the trustees voted "that automobiles be allowed in the cemetery grounds subject to such reasonable rules as the superintendent sees fit."

In 1920, the Soldiers Lot was laid out, though the land had been set aside by the cemetery trustees as early as 1896. It was thought that a lot for service men and women who had served in World War I could be interred in a central area like the lot for Civil War soldiers and veterans. Marked by a stone memorial with bronze tablets, it honors those from Milton who had served in the armed forces. Individual graves are marked by simple white marble markers and a central flagpole flies the United States flag. Seeking available land to expand the cemetery, the town in 1924 purchased land from J. Merrill Brown and land owned by the heirs of Merrill H. Brown. There would also be a Milton Police Monument and a Milton Firemen Monument for policemen and firemen established at this time.

The cemetery was enlarged in 1945 with the purchase of the 34-acre Ladd Estate on Centre Street. One section was the rear acreage of the estate of Alexander Haven Ladd, who was a cemetery trustee. The Ladd-Brooks Section was once a part of *Wayside Farm*, the estate of J. Henry Brooks, whose house was on Adams Street and the Alexander H. Ladd House on Centre Street which was destroyed by fire. This area, a level terrain that is bordered by mature trees, was developed in a more regulated design and height of headstones in 1946 with the laying out of Maple Avenue and two additional acres were added in 1961 along the Murray Avenue border. In the late 1990s the Copeland Garden was laid out as a circular formal garden, designed by Therese Desmond-Sills, in "a faux French Renaissance style of a contemplative garden to bury and memorialize cremated remains.… Cremations are buried beneath the flat bluestone steppingstones around the garden so that the design is not disturbed by the internments." This garden was planted with magnolia trees, lavender, David Austin yellow roses, ground cover and boxwood. Adjoining it is the Garden of Hope.

The Modern Cemetery, in the center of the cemetery, was laid out in 1945, in an area that was once part of Unquety Brook with three small ponds that had once provided a picturesque aspect to the cemetery. In 1970, the most drastic change in the topography of the Milton Cemetery took place when Unquety Brook, which flowed through the center of the cemetery, was put underground by a culvert that runs under Locust Avenue from the Duck Pond to Paradise Pond, and the land was infilled, graded, and developed as burial lots in a series of long rows with headstones of regulated height.

The Garden of Faith was laid out in the late twentieth century along the road accessed from Gun Hill Road, just under Pine Avenue. Here, mature trees had tree-wells created by slabs of granite, ironically some bearing the names of families when the tombs were removed from the Olde Burying Grounds in the late 1880s, used when the level of the land was raised and graded to provide new graves.

Perpetual care lawn cemeteries or memorial parks of the twentieth century represent a transformation of the "rural" cemetery ideal that began in the last half of the nineteenth century.

1
THE OLDE BURYING GROUNDS

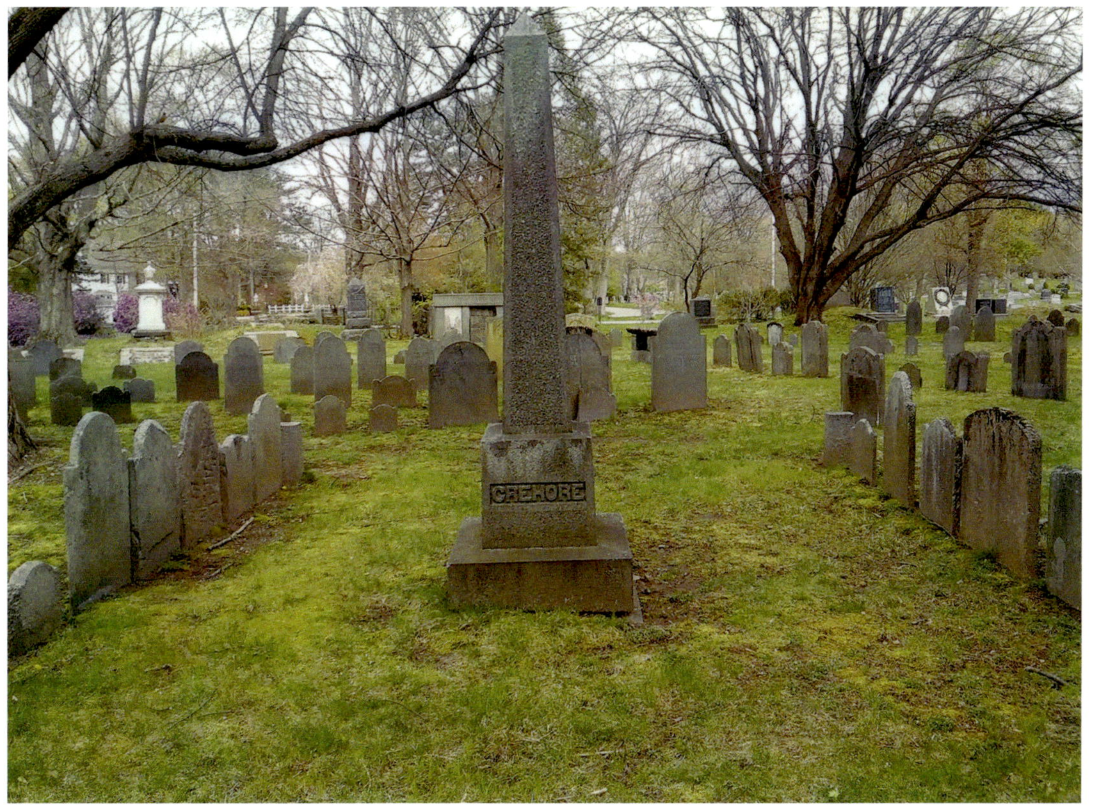

The grave of Teague Crehore dates to the late seventeenth century. Crehore hailed from Ireland and settled in Milton in 1645 and with Mary Spurr Crehore was the progenitor of generations of descendants who after their deaths were buried near his grave. A nineteenth-century granite obelisk on a plinth base is set in the center of the family lot with slate headstones lined shoulder to shoulder, from generation-to-generation perpetuating familial ties dating back to 1696. (*Photograph by Peter B. Kingman*)

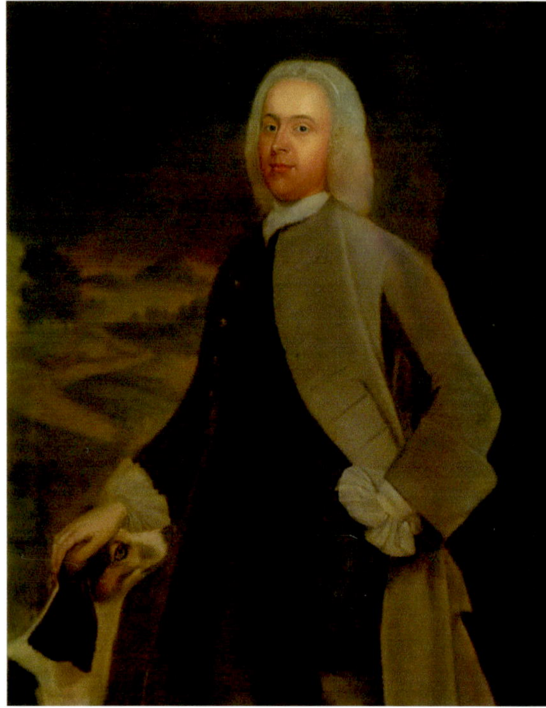

Oxenbridge Thacher, Jr. (1719–1765) attended Harvard and was the first Harvard freshman to receive the Hopkins Prize, named for Edward Hopkins. He was a founding member of the Society of Propagating Christian Knowledge Among the Indians of North America, a member of the Massachusetts Committee of Correspondence, and served as a member of the House of Representatives. Thacher and James Otis Jr. successfully argued the case in Massachusetts against the English Writs of Assistance, and John Adams credited Thacher as being one of the patriots who sparked the Revolution. Adams said the British "hated him worse than they did [James] Otis or Samuel Adams, and they feared him more." (*Collection of Yale University Art Gallery*)

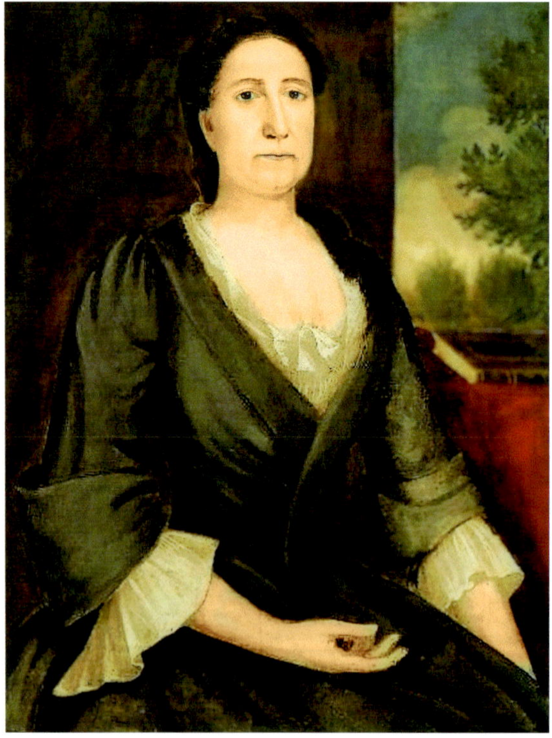

Madam Elizabeth Campbell Foye (1695–1782) was the widow of William Foye who served as treasurer of the Province of Massachusetts Bay. She and her daughters, Elizabeth Foye and Mary Foye Cooper, gave to the town of Milton in 1760 a half-acre and six rods of land for the price of one shilling. This was called the First Enlargement of the cemetery and would be the first of many additions of land. Her portrait was painted by Joseph Badger in 1750. (*Collection of Museum of Fine Arts*)

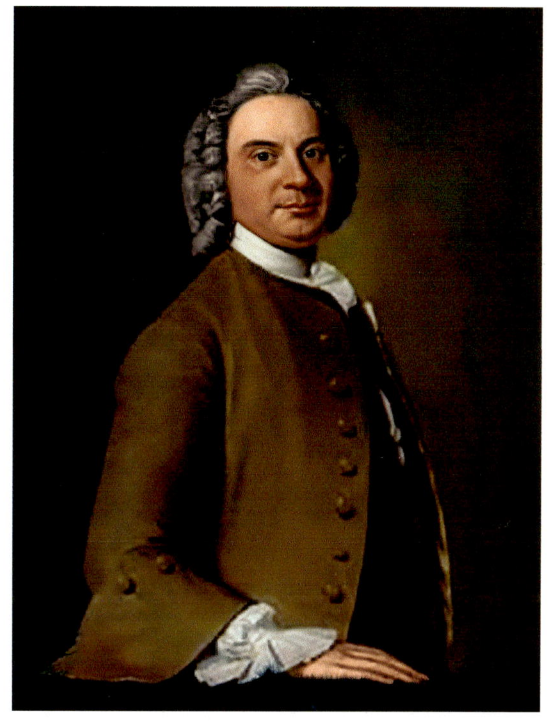

John Rowe (1715–1787) was a merchant in eighteenth-century Boston and was a member of the House of Representatives of the Province of Massachusetts Bay. He was a slave dealer as shown by his advertisement in the July 28, 1746, edition of the *Boston Evening Post.* He was also the owner of the *Eleanor,* one of the tea ships whose cargo of tea played a starring role in the Boston Tea Party. Today, his name is remembered to this day in Rowe's Wharf, a modern development in downtown Boston on the site of his original wharf. His portrait was painted in 1748 by John Feke. (*Collection of Gilcrease Museum*)

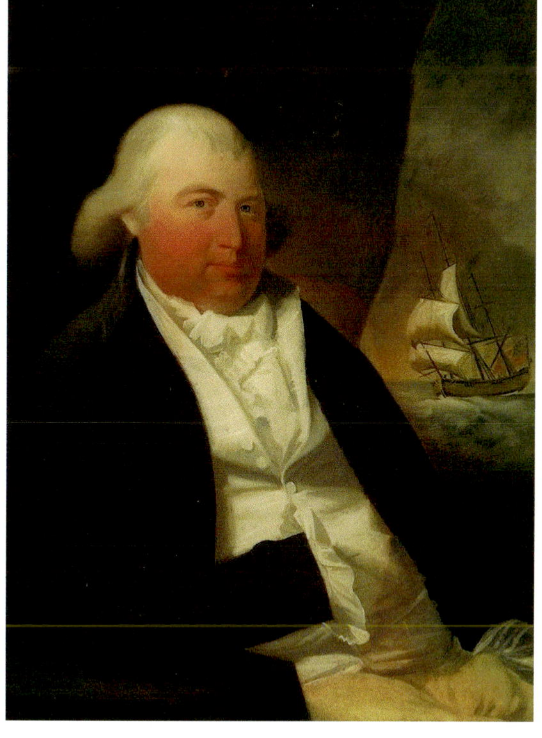

John McLean (1761–1823) was a merchant who partnered with Isaac Davenport with a fleet of ships that traded at ports across the globe. In 1823, he placed mile markers from Boston to Milton, Massachusetts and his business partner, Isaac Davenport, completed the work after McLean's death; he had McLean's name inscribed on the markers. His great claim to fame was that he left a bequest, as well as the residuary of his estate, to the Massachusetts General Hospital. The bequest and residue from McLean were the largest amount that was given to the hospital prior to 1851 and the McLean Asylum was named in his memory. McLean's portrait is by John Johnston showing one of his cargo ships traversing the ocean. (*Collection of Harvard Art Museums*)

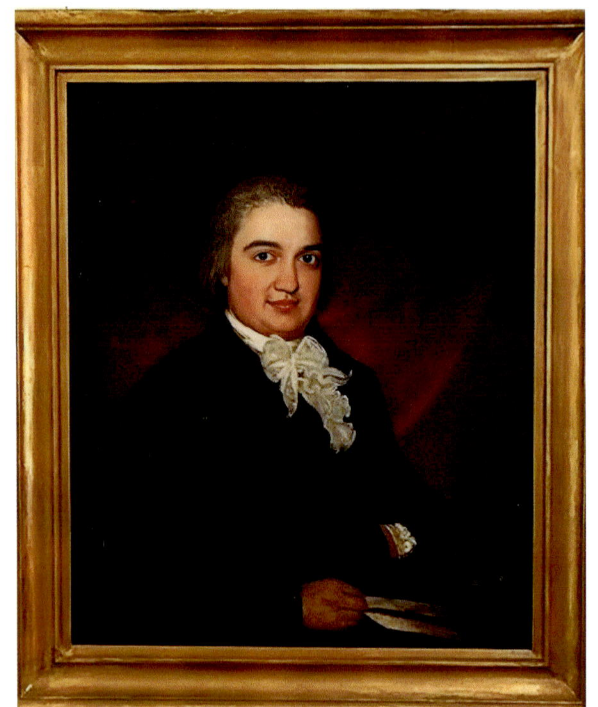

Jonathan Russell (1771–1832) graduated from Rhode Island College, now Brown University. He was said to have been "a versatile, forcible, elegant and facile writer" and engaged in the mercantile business in partnership with Otis Ammidon, importing goods from Europe. In 1811, Russell was appointed by President James Madison as *chargé d'affaires* in Paris, and he functioned as minister to France and later as *chargé d'affaires* and acting minister when war was declared by the United States in 1812. He was minister to Sweden and Norway from 1814–1818. Russell was one of the five commissioners who negotiated the Treaty of Ghent with Great Britain in 1814, which ended the War of 1812. "Jonathan Russell was buried on his own estate in what is now known as Hutchinson's Field. In 1855 his remains were removed to Forest Hills Cemetery and in 1887 removed back to Milton and inhumed in Milton Cemetery where the grave is marked by a suitably inscribed tombstone." (*Courtesy of Perry Russell*)

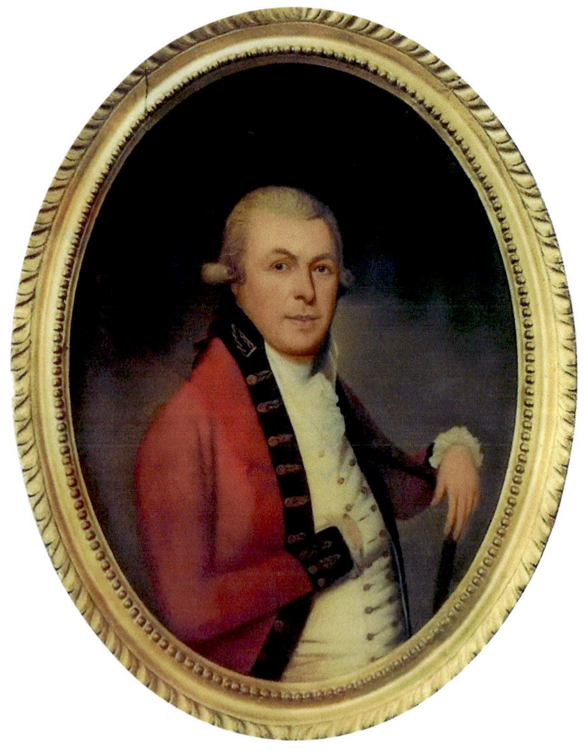

Thomas McDonogh (1740–1805) served as the private secretary to John Wentworth, the last royal governor of New Hampshire. McDonogh fled the colony with Wentworth in 1775 and was a loyalist refugee in Nova Scotia. Following the 1783 Peace of Paris, McDonogh was appointed British consul in Boston, and served in that office until his death. According to *The Wentworth Genealogy: English and American*, he was interred in the tomb of his daughter and son-in-law, Charlotte McDonogh and Peter Oxenbridge Thacher. (*Collection of the Museum of the American Revolution*)

2
CHOSE WHO SERVED

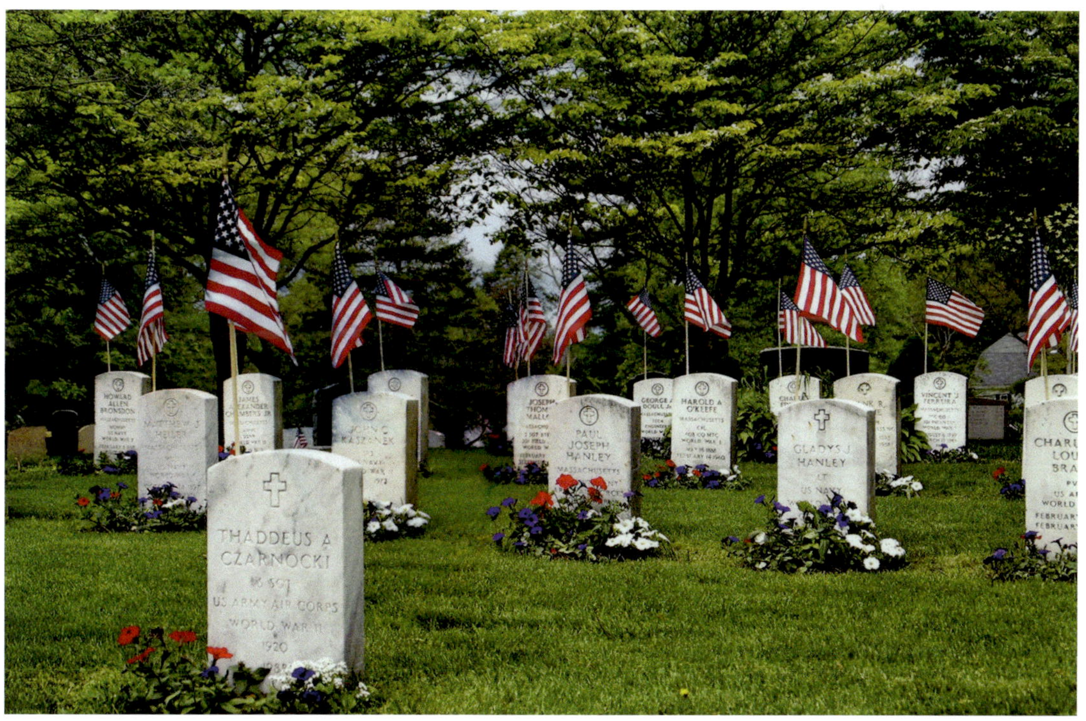

At the Veterans' Lot at Milton Cemetery, the simple white marble headstones of the men and women of Milton who served in the wars mark a quiet and solemn area. Here flags are seen waving from the tops of the headstones on Memorial Day. Following World War I, the United States government adopted a new design to be used for all veteran graves. The stone was of the slab design referred to as the "General" type, slightly rounded at the top, of American white marble and 42 inches high. The inscription on the front face would include the name of the soldier, his rank, regiment, division, date of death, and the state from which he came. (*Photograph by Peter B. Kingman*)
   Non sibi sed Patriae.

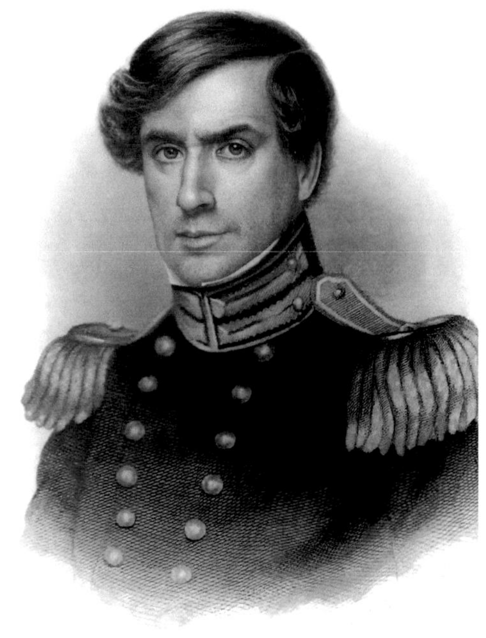

First Lieutenant Josiah Howe Vose, Jr. (1815–1841) was the son of Colonel Josiah Howe and Charlotte Cushing Vose and received a commission in the United States Army in 1837. He served in the Seminole War in Florida which arose through disputes over land, trade, and slavery. The United States wanted the land on which the Seminoles lived, but the Seminole refused to leave. The result was that the United States voided the Treaty of Moultrie Creek and demanded that all Seminoles relocate to Indian Territory in present-day Oklahoma under the Indian Removal Act. Vose served in the Everglades swampland in Florida and exposure brought on consumption, and he died in New York.

In the midst of life we are in death.

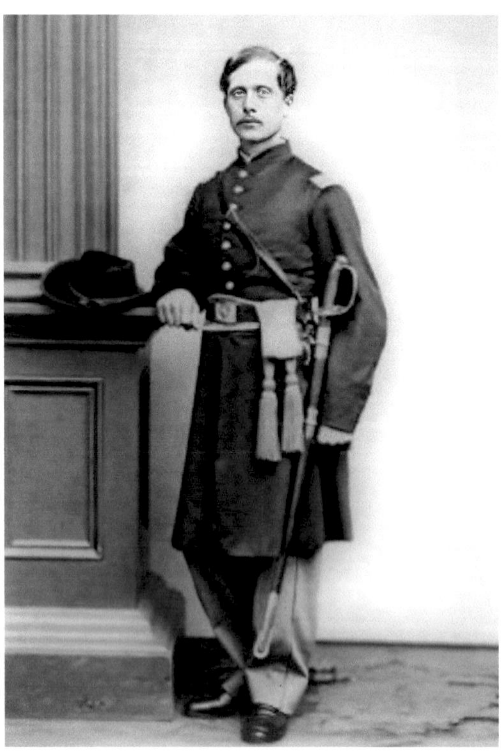

James Francis Pope (1845–1920) served as a drummer boy in Company A, 13th Massachusetts Regiment, in the Civil War before joining the 123rd Regiment, Massachusetts Infantry. Captured at the Battle of Gettysburg, he was imprisoned for two years at Libbey Prison and later Belle Island. After the Civil War, he was co-owner with Jacob A. Turner of the Pope and Turner Ice Company on the Blue Hills Parkway, where the company employed twelve men for six months of the year and fifteen horses to score and cut the pond ice. The icehouses required the services of 100 men to cut and store the ice, securing about 1,000 tons of ice each day during the winter. In the days before electric freezers, icehouses were invaluable to a community.

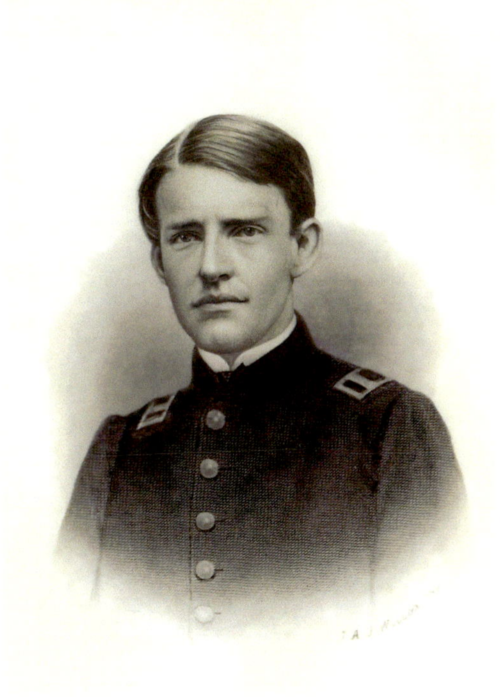

Lieutenant Josiah Howe Vose Field (1843–1864) attended Milton Academy and graduated from West Point in 1863. He enlisted in the army during the Civil War and served as senior ordinance officer for Western Virginia and attended General Hunter in his raid through Virginia. In a letter he wrote to his family, he said, "I am played out and exhausted, but my courage is good; I would not have missed this raid." He died at Cumberland, Maryland.

*He, the young and strong, who
cherished Noble longings for the strife,
    By the wayside fell and perished,
Weary with the march of life.*

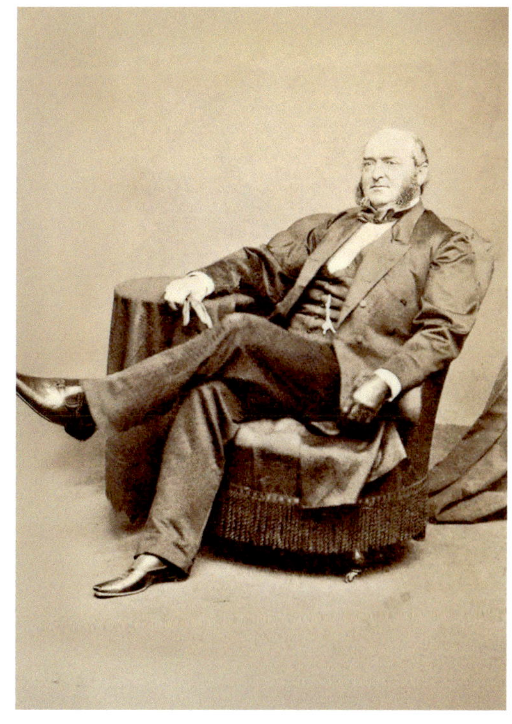

Dr. Christopher Columbus Holmes (1817–1882) served as colonel of the First Corps Cadets. During the Civil War, the cadets reported to Fort Warren in Boston Harbor where they guarded Confederate prisoners and wore the standard peacetime grey field uniform of the Massachusetts Volunteer Militia. While in federal service, the corps was issued the standard blue army uniform. During the service of the 45th, the corps, minus most of its members, remained in state service as a home guard unit. The corps, in effect, performed two missions during the Civil War: it provided officers for new units while older cadets remained in Boston for state service. Holmes was a well-known physician in Milton.

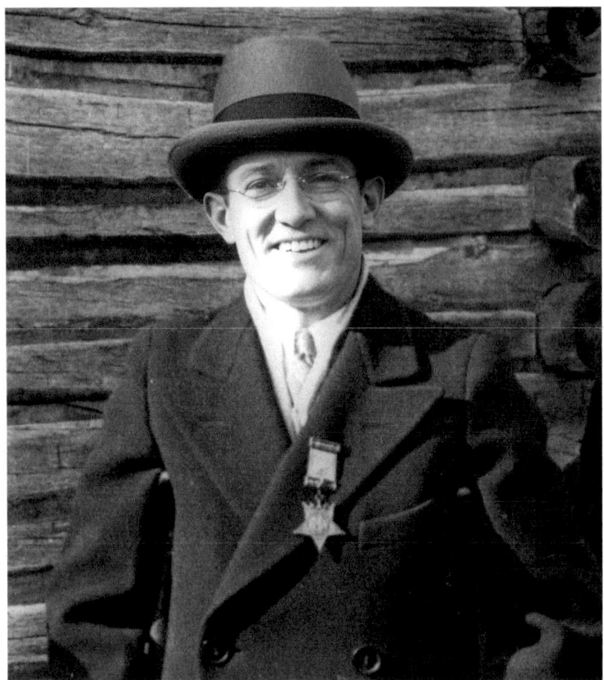

Edward Allen Gisburne (1892–1955) was a United States Navy officer and a recipient of the U.S. military's highest decoration, the Medal of Honor, for his role in the battle which began the United States occupation of Veracruz, Mexico. He earned the medal as an enlisted man for ignoring heavy fire and his own severe injuries to drag a wounded marine to safety. Although he lost his left leg in the fight, he went on to complete two more terms of service with the navy, one as a radio operator during World War I and another as a fifty-year-old commissioned officer in World War II.

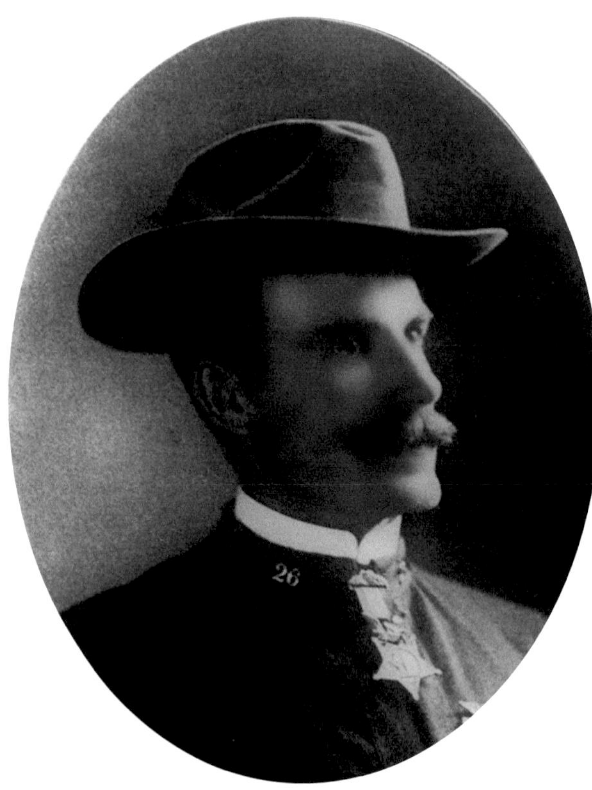

Corporal Paul Weinert (1869–1919) was a soldier in the United States Army who served with the 1st U.S. Artillery during the Indian Wars and was present at the Wounded Knee Massacre when, on the morning of December 29, 1890, members of the 7th U.S. Cavalry Regiment surrounded the camp of the Sioux chieftain Big Foot to apprehend weapons from his band. Weinert was one of twenty men who received the Medal of Honor for gallantry at what was then called the Battle of Wounded Knee, but now commonly referred to as the Wounded Knee Massacre. The citation read "Taking the place of his commanding officer who had fallen severely wounded, he gallantly served his piece, after each fire advancing it to a better position."

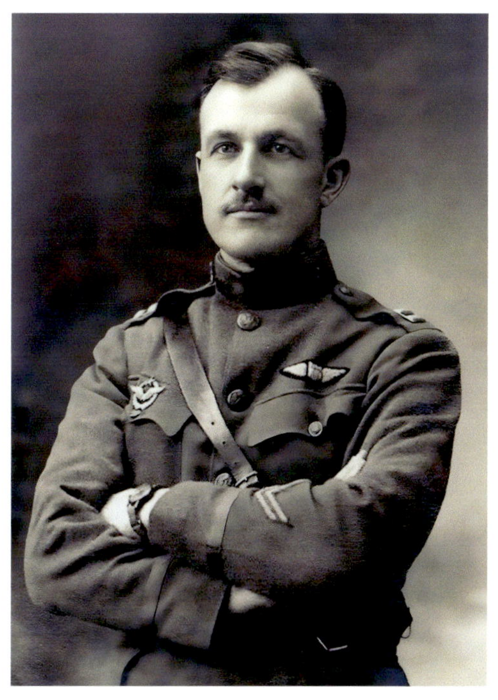

Gerrit Forbes (1880–1964) attended Harvard and studied aeronautics at the Provincial Aviation School in London, with Messrs. Warren and Smiles on a 45-hp two-seater biplane. World War I would pioneer new forms of combat, including the first-ever encounters in the sky as fighter pilots fought high above the battlefields of Europe for dominance over the enemy. Forbes is seen wearing the December 1917 Military Aviator Badge on his tunic as well as his circular pilot medal.

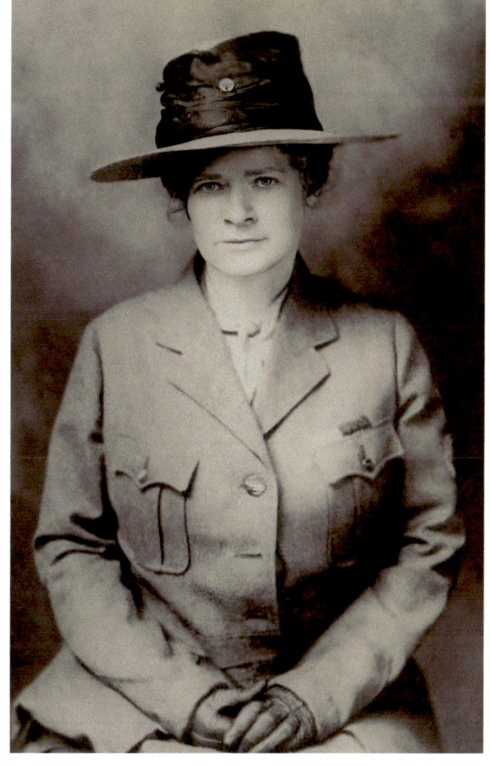

Amelia Peabody Tileston (1872–1920) was the daughter of John Boies Tileston whose estate Briarfield was near Eliot Street and Blue Hills Parkway. She studied nursing and devoted her life, tirelessly, to aid people who were suffering. She traveled the world to this end, and in 1916, returning from Europe, was consumed by wanting to aid the beleaguered Serbian refugees from World War I. She went to Serbia and worked for the Red Cross but died there of pneumonia. The book *Amelia Peabody Tileston and Her Canteens for the Serbs*, written by her mother, Mary Wilder Foote Tileston (1843–1934), recounted the hard life of soldiers in camp, and her daughter's devotion to duty.

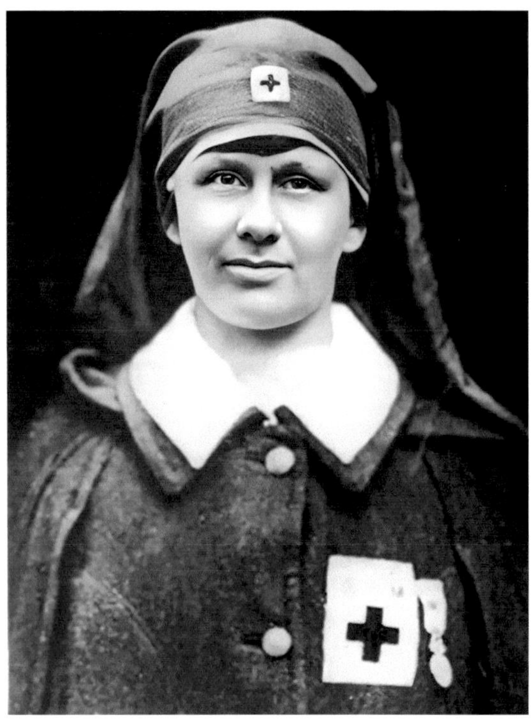

Helen Homans (1884–1918) became a nurse in France in 1915 and stayed there throughout World War I until her death from influenza, a little less than a week before the Armistice. Shortly before her death in Pontoise, Departement du Val-d'Oise, Île-de-France, she was awarded the Croix de Guerre by the head of the French medical staff. On her coffin plate was engraved "MORTE POUR LA FRANCE" (Dead for France). Her medical colleagues had fought to keep her alive, and she herself had struggled valiantly. A fellow nurse from Boston, Edith Parkman, said of Homans "Everybody who saw her at work, doctors, nurses … appreciated that she literally killed herself for her wounded."

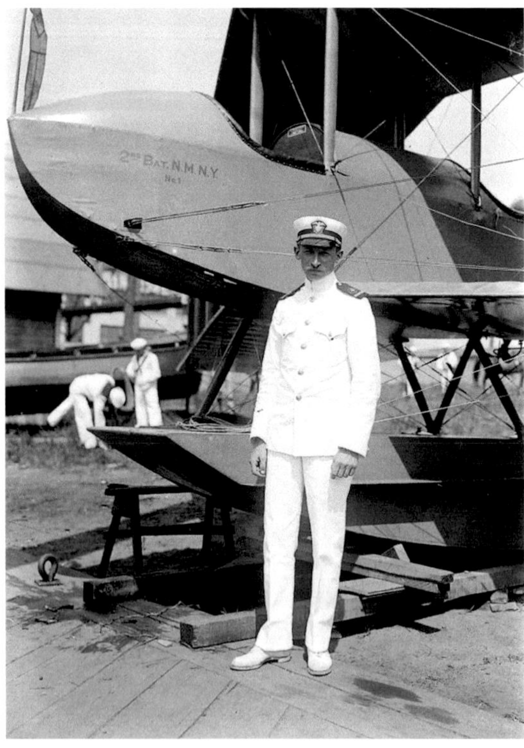

Ensign Samuel Stillman Pierce (1887–1962) attended Volkmann's School and the Massachusetts Institute of Technology. He was an aeroengineer and aviator and served as a flight instructor during World War I, working at the Naval Aircraft Factory in Philadelphia. He later worked in France for Blériot Aéronautique as "mechanic, test pilot, instructor and translator of foreign correspondence." His work included missions abroad to organize the Royal Serbian Flying Corps during the First Balkan War, to set up a flying school in Egypt, and to prepare Lieutenant Tryggve Gran in Scotland for a flight across the North Sea. He would establish the S. S. Pierce Aeroplane Corporation in New York. He was a teacher for many years at Milton Academy. (*Courtesy Polly Pillsbury*)

James Handasyd Perkins (1876–1940) attended Milton Academy and Harvard. He served in France during World War I and in 1918 was given complete charge of this country's European Red Cross organization. In September of that year, he was made a lieutenant colonel in the American Expeditionary Force and was assigned to General Headquarters at Chaumont, France, as assistant chief of staff of the Second Army, later of the Third Army or the Army of Occupation at Coblenz. The many decorations awarded to Perkins in World War I were Ordre national de la Légion d' Honneur, the Distinguished Service Medal, and the Belgian Decoration of Croix de Commandeur de l' Ordre de la Couronne. He later became chairman of National City Bank, later chairman of Citigroup.

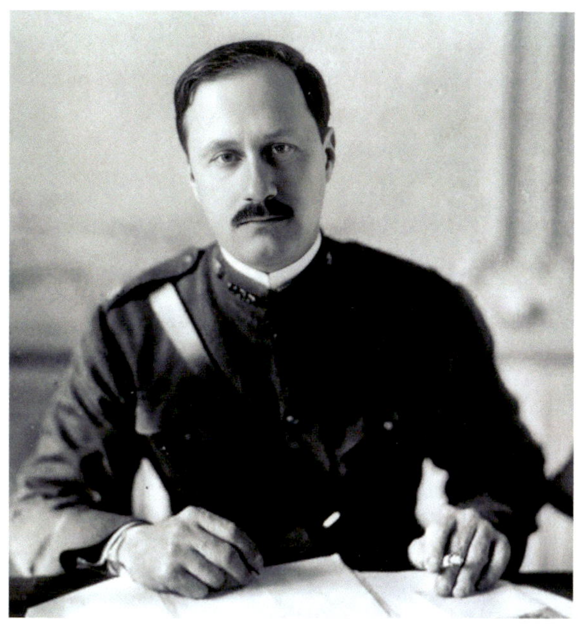

Dwight Durkee Evans, Jr. (1921–1968) graduated from Milton Academy and Harvard University. He entered the Army Air Corps in 1942 and served with the 15th Air Corps in Africa and Italy as a combat navigator on a B-24 bomber. He was awarded the Air Medal with three clusters and served in four campaigns overseas. He later completed pilot training and served as intelligence officer and pilot with the Strategic Air Command during the Korean War and was a lieutenant colonel in the Air Force Reserve. He later served as an officer of the First National Bank of Boston, a trustee of the China Trade Museum, and was a president of the Milton Historical Society. (*Courtesy of Mary Eliza Kimball*)

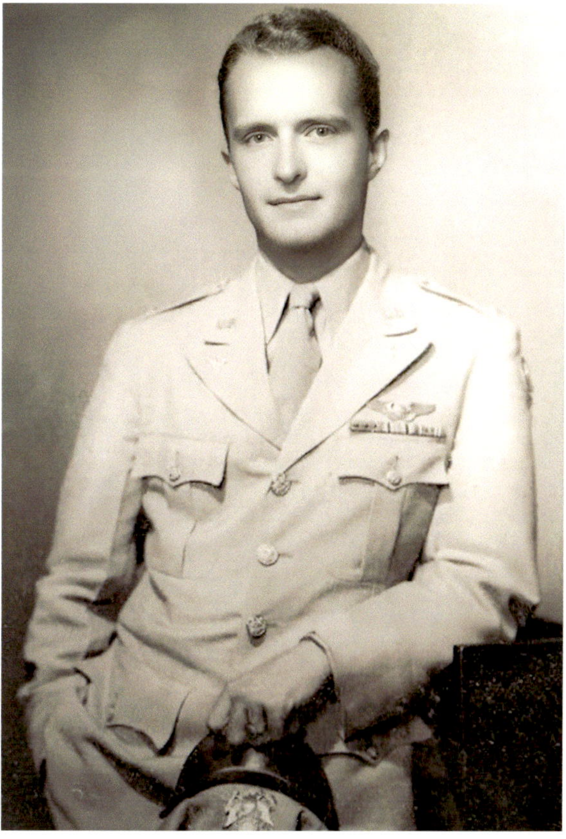

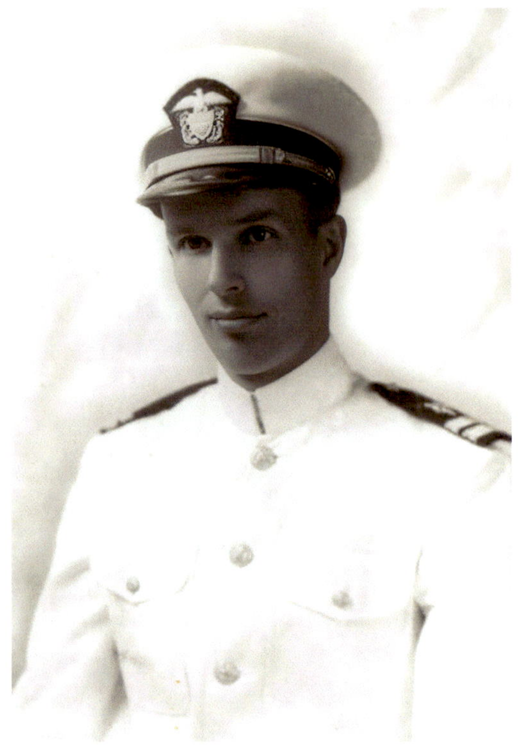

Henry Bigelow Jackson (1906–1995) served as an officer in the United States Navy during World War II. He graduated from Harvard University and joined the faculty at Belmont Hill School. He served as the school's business manager and was chair of the mathematics department. In 1988, he was awarded the Milton Medal, Milton Academy's highest honor and an expression of the school's deep gratitude to those graduates who have contributed the most to their community.

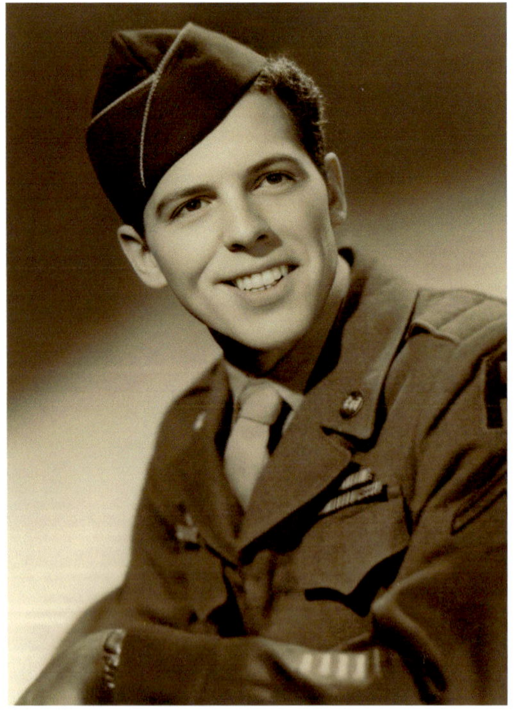

During World War II, Joseph Clifford Theriault (1923–2013) served with 234th Engineer Combat Battalion and participated in the D-Day landings on Omaha Beach, Normandy, and received the Purple Heart on the Siegfried Line. He was a union carpenter and was employed by Thomas O'Connor Construction Company, where he was involved with the restoration of St. Stephen's Church (formerly the New North Church) and the Old North Church in Boston's North End.

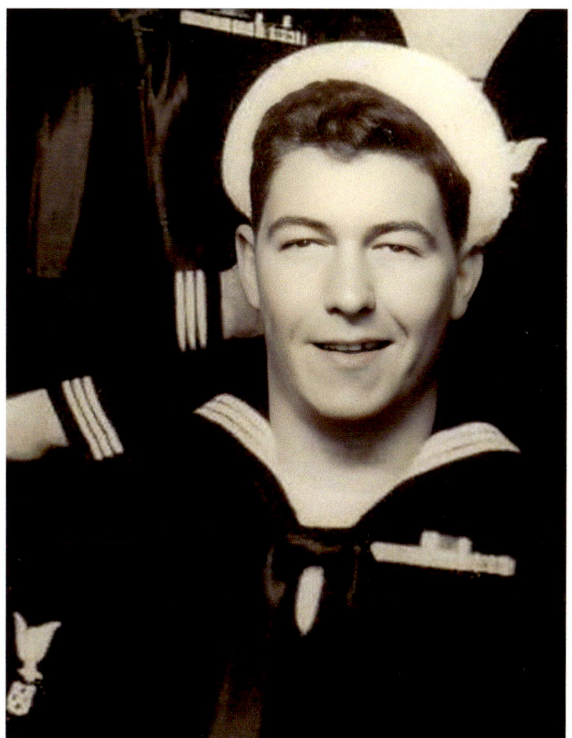

Thomas Francis Williams (1923–2006) entered the navy in 1942 and served as a coxswain on an LCVP landing craft. He participated in the first wave D-Day assault on Normandy and three other invasions. He received several decorations and was discharged in 1945 as a boatswain's mate, second class. He was a member of Pipe Fitters Local No. 537 of Boston and co-owner of the Fred Williams Inc. of Randolph, Massachusetts.

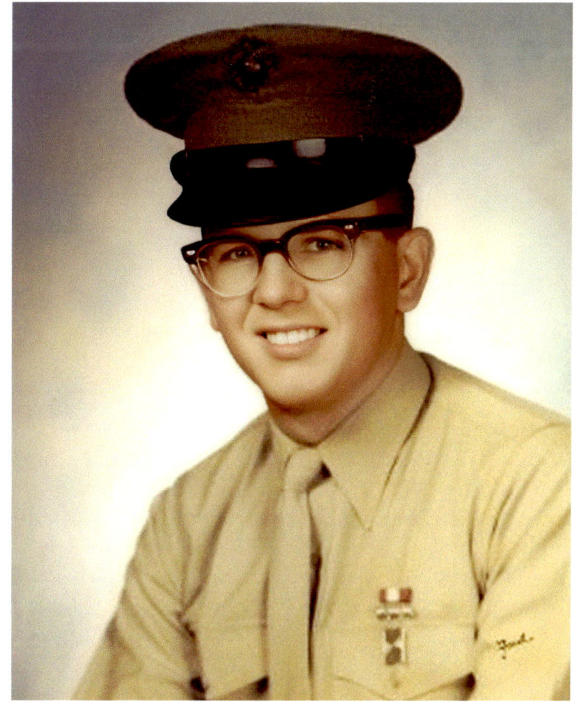

Corporal Joseph D. McNeil, USMC (1947–1968) enlisted in the U.S. Marine Corps in 1966. He was deployed to Vietnam on January 13, 1967, where he was assigned for duty with Company B, 3rd AMTRAC Battalion, 1st MARDIV (Rein) FMF. While in Duy Xuyen District of Quang Nam Province Korea, McNeil was struck by lightning as he was returning from a vehicle to his own LVT. He was immediately given first aid and evacuated but was declared dead on arrival at the NSA Hospital in Da Nang, Vietnam.

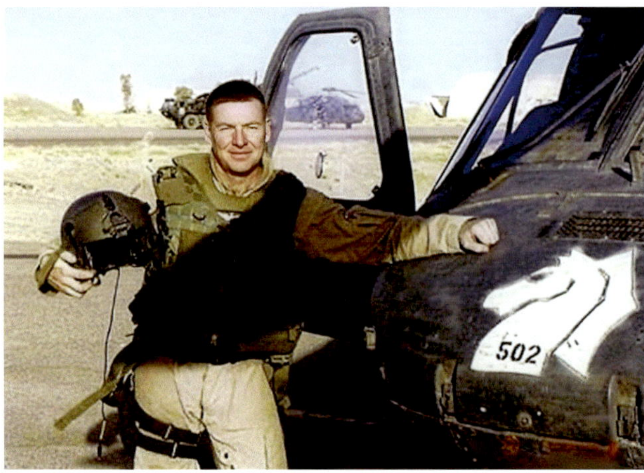

Army Chief Warrant Officer 3 Kyran E. Kennedy (1960–2003) was a member of the 5th Battalion, 101st Aviation Regiment, 101st Airborne Division (Air Assault), Fort Campbell, KY, which had been deployed to Iraq for Operation Iraqi Freedom. He had been commended for his ingenuity as a safety officer, finding safer ways to accomplish his unit's goals. He was killed in 2003, when his UH-60 Black Hawk helicopter was shot down in Tikrit, Iraq, during Operation Iraqi Freedom. He was awarded the Bronze Star, Air Medal, Purple Heart, National Defense, Iraq Campaign, and the Global War on Terror. The Kyran E. Kennedy Award was established in his memory at UMass Boston to provide financial support to a full-time student, with preference afforded to a student who is a veteran or active-duty member of the military.

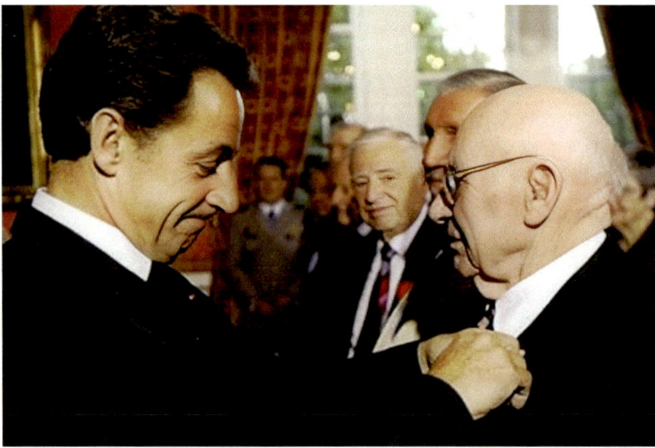

France's President Nicolas Sarkozy awards the Chevalier de la Legion d' Honneur medal to U.S. World War II veteran George Thompson (1925–2016). Thompson had served in the U.S. Army's 90th Infantry Division and was part of the Normandy invasion, landing on Utah Beach on D-Day+2, and was awarded the Bronze Star and the Purple Heart for his service. He took part in a nighttime rescue of American soldiers across the Moselle River in Germany in November 1944. He also fought in the Battle of the Bulge and was one of the liberators of the Flossenburg concentration camp in Germany, which primarily housed political prisoners and prisoners of war.

3

BUSINESSES, MANUFACTURERS, MAGNATES

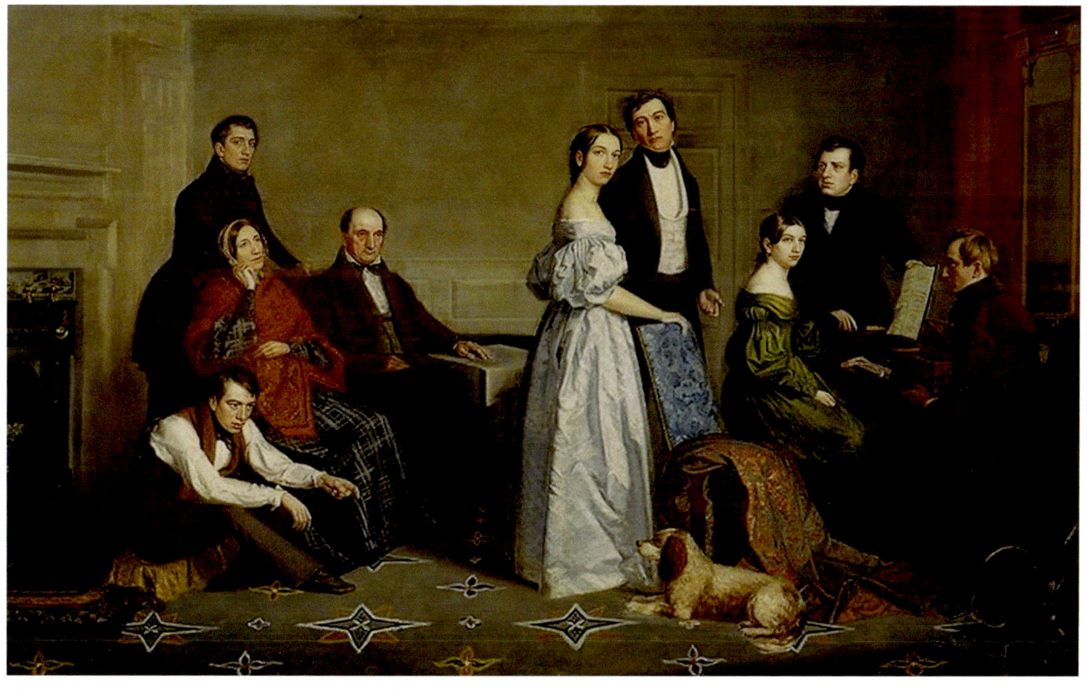

The Hollingsworth Family was painted by George Hollingsworth (1813–1882) in the family home on Brush Hill Road in Milton. Hollingsworth painted a scene of a comfortable evening in the parlor, with his family grouped around a pianoforte and his parents seated before the fireplace. Seen in the center are Mark and Waitstill Tileston Hollingsworth surrounded by their children, George, Anderson, Maria, John Mark, Cornelia, Amor, and Lyman Hollingsworth. Mark Hollingsworth was partner of Edmund P. Tileston in the Tileston & Hollingsworth Paper Mill. (*Collection of Museum of Fine Arts, Boston*)

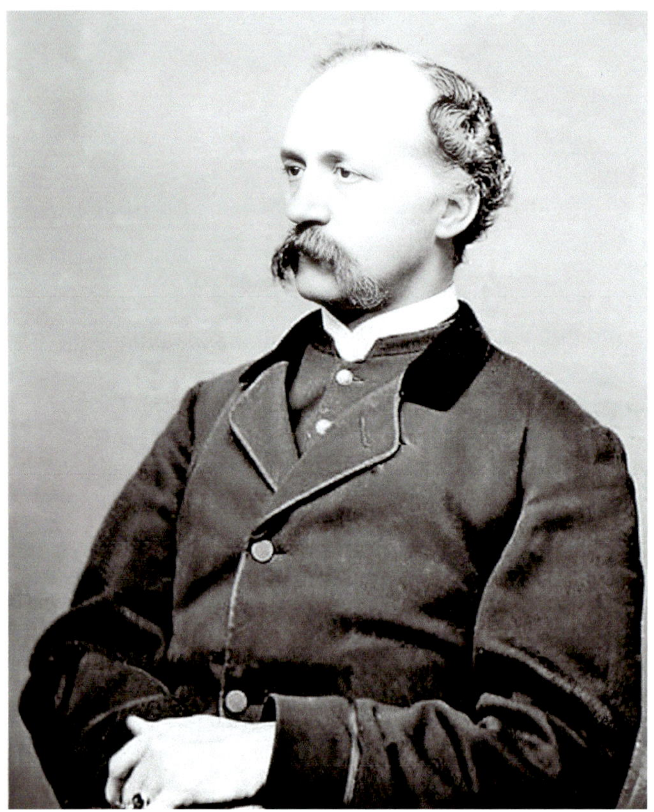

Alpheus Babcock (1785–1842), who learned his trade from musical instrument maker Benjamin Crehore (1765–1832) in Milton Village, was a piano and musical instrument maker who is known for patenting a complete iron frame in a single casting used to resist the strain of the strings in square pianos. He also patented what he called cross stringing and introduced resilient cloth hammer coverings. Later in his career he worked for Jonas Chickering and Babcock's improvements helped Chickering to become the leader of the American piano industry through the 1860s.

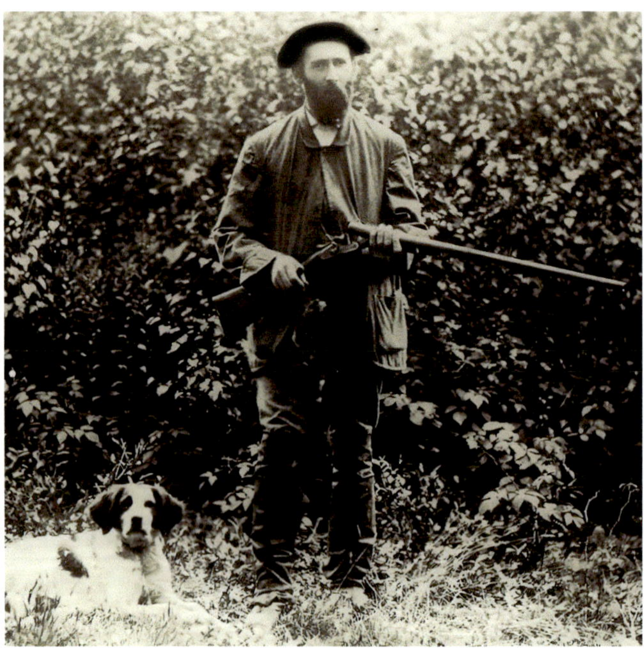

George H. Bent (1843–1915), seen with his Gordon setter "Water Cracker," was the grandson of Josiah Bent who in 1801 began baking water crackers, which are biscuits made of flour and water that crackled when put to a hot fire, thus he created the cracker. These hard crackers had shelf life and would not deteriorate during long sea voyages. In the 1860s, the company sold the original hardtack crackers used by troops during the American Civil War. In 1898, Bent joined the National Biscuit Company, which now does business under the Nabisco name. (*Courtesy of Dennis "Mike" Doyle*)

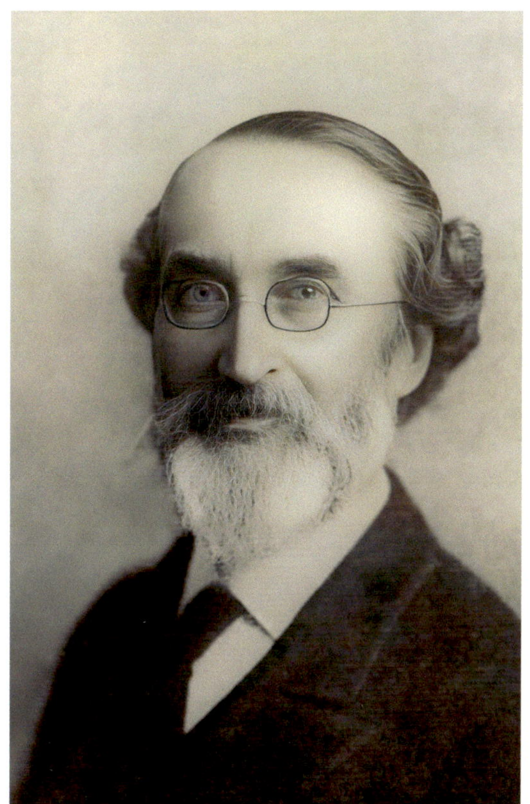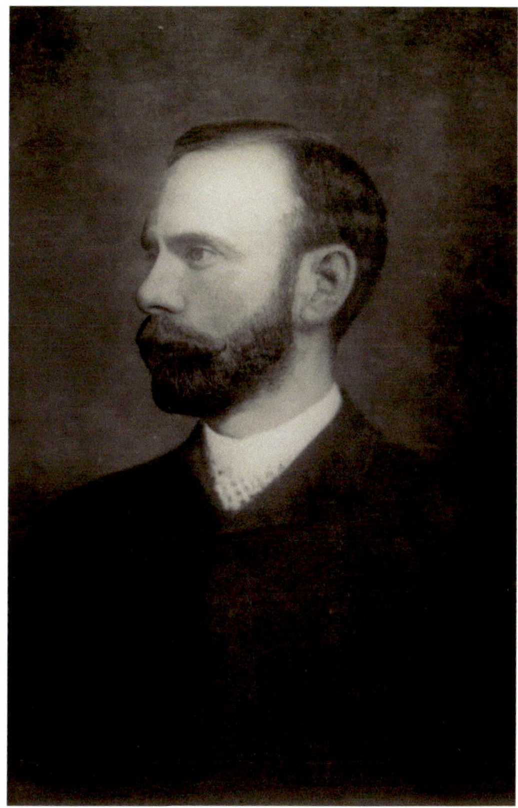

Above left: George Harvey Chickering (1830–1899) was the son of Jonas Chickering who in 1823 began making pianos. Chickering was the largest piano manufacturer in the United States in the middle of the nineteenth century but was surpassed in the 1860s by Steinway. In 1908, the company became part of the American Piano Company and continued after the merger in 1932 of American with the Aeolian Company, to form Aeolian-American. That company went out of business in 1985, but the Chickering name continued to be applied to new pianos produced by Wurlitzer and then the Baldwin Piano Company.

Above right: Albert E. Touzalin (1842–1889) was the general land agent of the Atchison, Topeka, and Santa Fe Railroad remaining until 1875 when he became general land agent in Nebraska and Iowa for Burlington. In 1878, he was made general manager of the Burlington and Missouri Railroad in Nebraska, and in 1881, he became vice-president of the consolidated lines in Nebraska and Iowa. In 1883, he was elected vice-president of the Atchison, Topeka, and Santa Fe, which office he held for one year when ill health caused him to resign. Two years later, he undertook the project of building the Chicago, Burlington & Northern Railroad from Chicago to St. Paul. He completed the project, organized the company, and was elected its first president. Touzalin formed the Montecito Land Company 1887 and sold lots for development; The American Riviera, as Montecito is referred to, evolved into an exclusive area in the twentieth century. (*Courtesy of Douglas County Historical Society*)

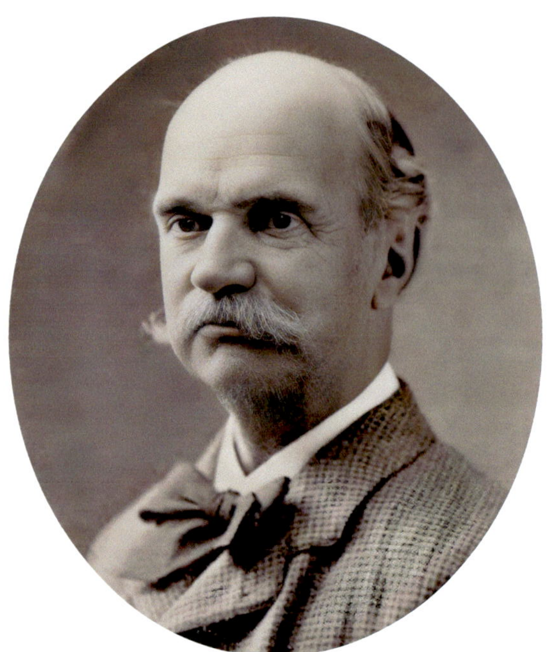 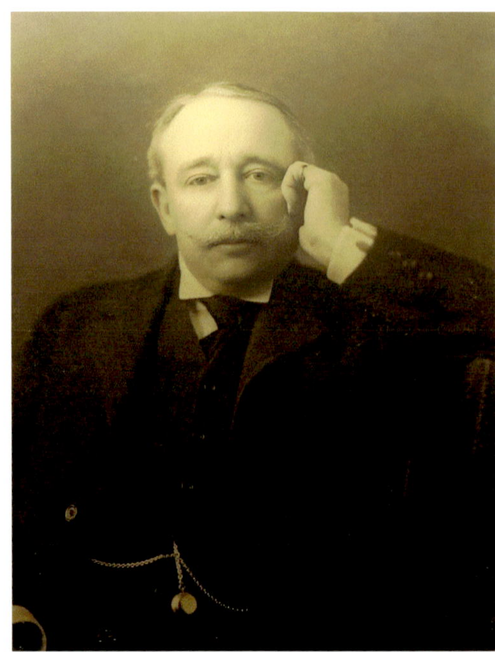

Above left: Henry Sturgis Russell (1838–1905) graduated from Harvard. During the Civil War, he served as lieutenant colonel in the 2nd Massachusetts Cavalry. In 1864, he was made a colonel of the 5th Regiment Massachusetts Colored Volunteer Cavalry and was brevetted brigadier general in 1865. After the war, Russell joined J. M. Forbes & Co., where he sold goods from China and East India. He was to serve as commissioner of the Boston Police Department and commissioner of the Boston Fire Department. His estate was Home Farm, and he had a horse stud there where he bred the great champion trotting stallion Smuggler. In 1909, a horse trough was erected opposite the Milton Public Library in memory of Russell.

Above right: Wallace Lincoln Pierce (1853–1920) was the son of Samuel Stillman and Ellen Maria Theresa Wallis Pierce and served as president of S. S. Pierce & Company from 1880–1920. He graduated from Boston English High School, and then entered the family business in 1871. In 1874, he was admitted to partnership in the company, and when the business was incorporated as S. S. Pierce Company, Wallace Lincoln Pierce became president and held the office until his death. With its own coat of arms adorning a distinctive red label on canned goods with the motto "Puritas et Cura" and the largest line of privately packed fancy foods in the world, S. S. Pierce & Company sold its wide assortment of delicacies not only at eight New England stores but through distributors across the United States and worldwide by mail order. (*Author's collection*)

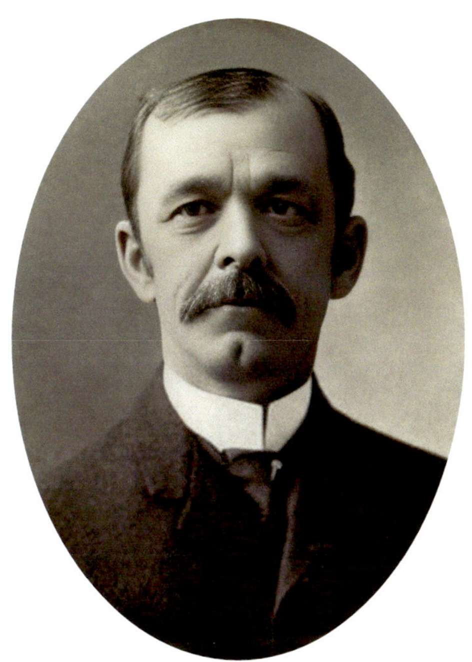 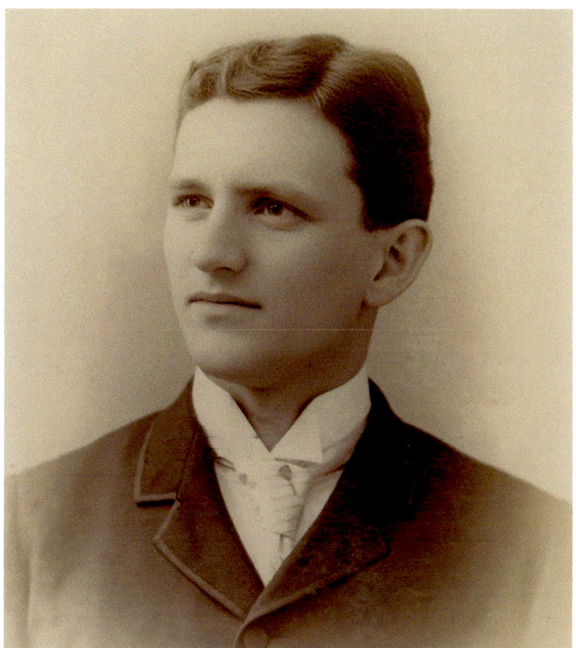

Above left: Hugh Clifford Gallagher (1855–1931) obtained an office position with Josiah Webb & Company in Milton Village in 1878, where "he became thoroughly familiar with manufacturing processes." In 1881, the company was sold to Henry L. Pierce and incorporated into the burgeoning Baker Chocolate Company. Gallagher became superintendent under Pierce until 1896, when he became vice-president in charge of manufacturing. In 1903, he became president of Walter Baker & Company, Ltd. He served in that capacity until 1926, when he was elected chairman of the board. Gallagher also served as a trustee of Boston University and was president of the Milton Savings Bank. (*Courtesy of Boston University, Howard Gotlieb Archival Research Center*)

Above right: William B. Thurber (1867–1937) graduated from the Massachusetts Institute of Technology in 1889 and served as a trustee and treasurer of the college from 1909–1913. He initially worked for the New England Telephone & Telegraph Company, but in 1898, he was hired as superintendent at Walter Baker & Company. Thurber served as president of Walter Baker & Company, Ltd., from 1926–1938, later serving as chairman of the board of directors. He supported several charities in Milton and served on the Milton School Committee; he was president of the Milton Hospital, chair of the Milton Red Cross, treasurer of Milton Academy and vice-president of the Blue Hill Bank & Trust Company. (*Courtesy of MIT*)

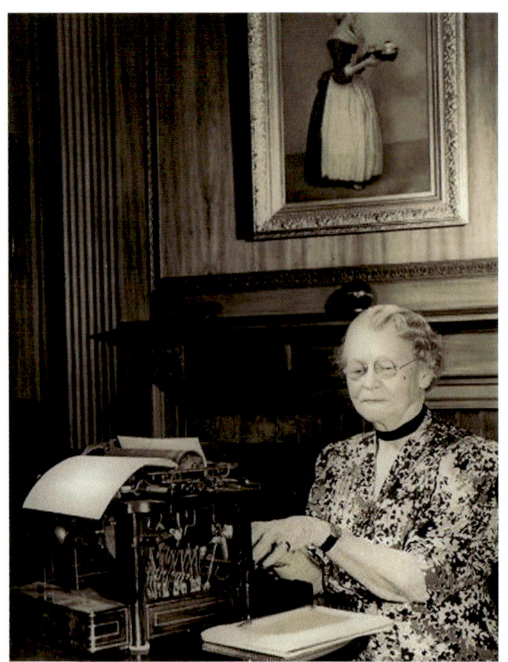 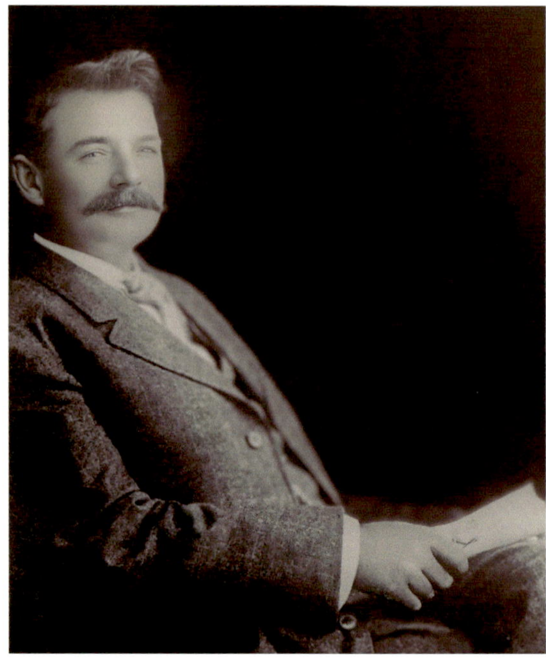

Above left: Clara Sophia Brown Pinckney (1856–1953) was employed in 1892 as the first woman stenographer at the Baker Chocolate Company and remained the only such employee for the next fifteen years. In 1919, when the new administration building was completed, the factory office force and the office force from Boston moved into new offices. Miss Pinckney was given a private office on the second-floor front and remained there for thirty-seven years, until her retirement in 1929. A dutiful and dedicated employee, she said in 1940 that she could not "remember in my time that any special effort was made to manufacture new products. Their line was well known, and, of course, at that time, there was not the strong competition which exists today." The office staff increased steadily so that by 1940, only five decades after she was first employed, there were about 100 young women employed in the administration building. (*Author's collection*)

Above right: Alexander Ambrose Will (1856–1910) was born in Clackriach, Old Deer, Scotland. Seeking greater opportunity, he immigrated on his own at the age of sixteen to Boston and settled in Milton. In 1886, he founded a general contracting business, A. A. Will Corp., on Blue Hill Avenue, adapting his knowledge of Scottish farm work to provide a wide range of useful services. In addition to building stone walls and general landscaping maintenance, the company offered teams of horses and tip carts for hire and the delivery of fill, firewood, and manure. Now in its fifth generation, A. A. Will Corp. is the oldest family-operated construction firm in the greater Boston area. (*Courtesy of Anthony Will*)

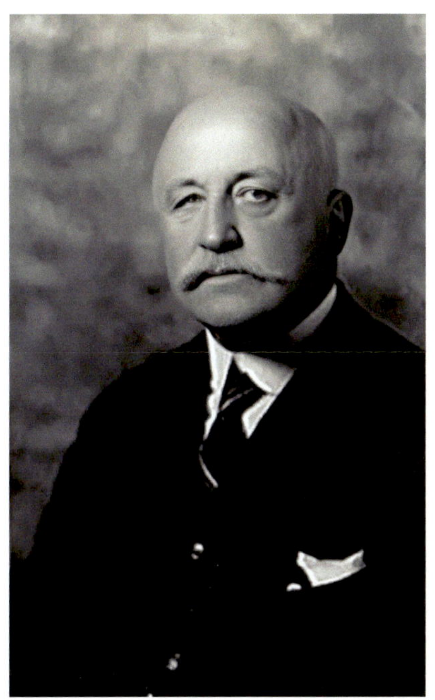 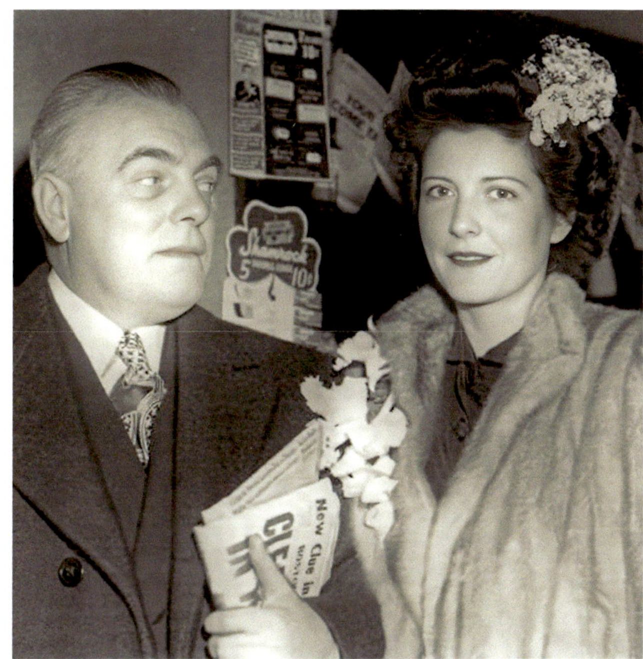

Above left: Galen Luther Stone (1862–1926) was the founder with Charles Hayden of Hayden, Stone & Co. of Boston. Stone was the financial editor of the *Boston Advertiser*, and he became apprentice, to acquire practical experience, in a brokerage firm. Hayden, Stone & Co was the greatest group of copper producing companies in the world owes its existence. In 1900, he and his associates formed the Eastern Steamship Lines, and he was honored for his philanthropy by initiation as an honorary member of Phi Mu Alpha Sinfonia fraternity in 1917 at the New England Conservatory of Music in Boston. Stone's philanthropy benefited Wellesley College, Harvard University, the Boston Symphony, and Massachusetts General Hospital, as well as museums and cultural organizations.

Above right: Howard Deering Johnson (1897–1972), seen with his fourth wife, Marjorie Smith Burgin Johnson (1911–2005,) created an orange-roofed empire of restaurants serving twenty-eight flavors of ice cream that would stretch from Maine to Florida and from the East Coast to the West Coast. The attractive white Colonial Revival restaurants, with eye-catching orange porcelain tile roofs, illuminated cupolas, and sea blue shutters, were described in *Reader's Digest* in 1949 as the epitome of "eating places that look like New England town meeting houses dressed up for Sunday." Known as the father of the "franchise industry," Johnson would revolutionize the restaurant industry in the United States and thereby ensure the delicious foods and quality prices that brought appreciative customers back for more. (*Author's collection*)

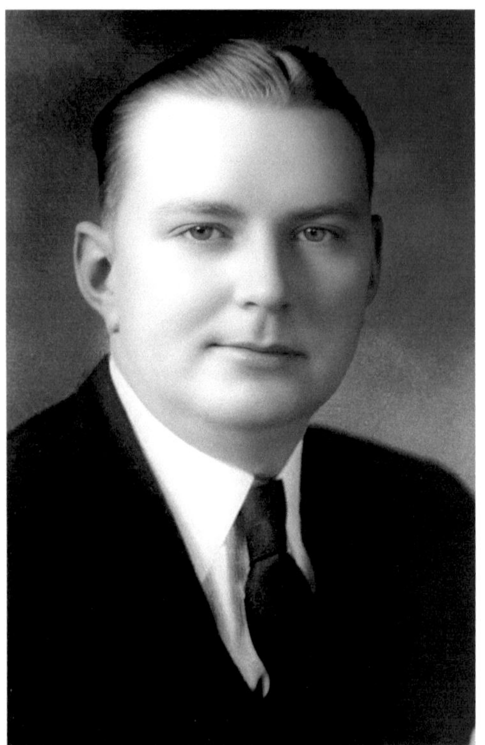 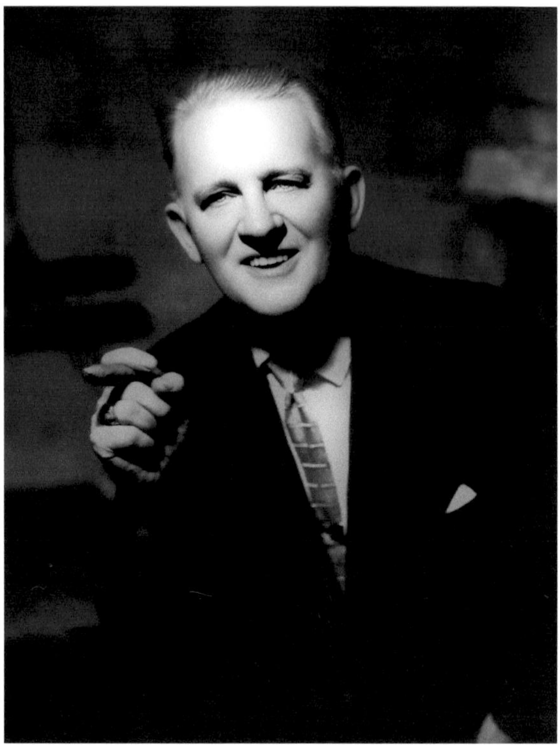

Above left: Lawrence Daniel Dunn (1904–1949) graduated from Boston College and served as a lieutenant in the navy during World War II. He was the president of the D. W. Dunn Company, a Boston movers and storage company which was founded in 1897 by his father, Daniel Webster Dunn, who served as president and treasurer. Dunn Movers was a local and long-distance moving company, packers, shippers, and offered warehouse storage. The Suffolk Storage Warehouse Company in Roxbury was also part of the Dunn Company and offered storage in separately locked rooms. (*Courtesy of Hannah Dray Vokey*)

Above right: Thomas English (1899–1988) was a native of Limerick, Ireland, and a well-known purveyor of libations at his welcoming pubs. His first pub was The Wigwam in Codman Square in Dorchester, a short distance from his home. The name came from the Boston Bees, as the baseball team the Boston Braves was known from 1936–1940; their baseball field off Commonwealth Avenue was called the Wigwam as Boston's NL franchise just wanted to stir the honey pot. Over the years, English's welcoming attitude, business acumen, and savvy saw the expansion of his pubs that he and later his family owned and operated throughout the city of Boston including Dorchester, West Roxbury, Hyde Park, Mattapan, Mission Hill, and South Boston, as well as Quincy and Cambridge. (*Courtesy of Mary Ann English*)

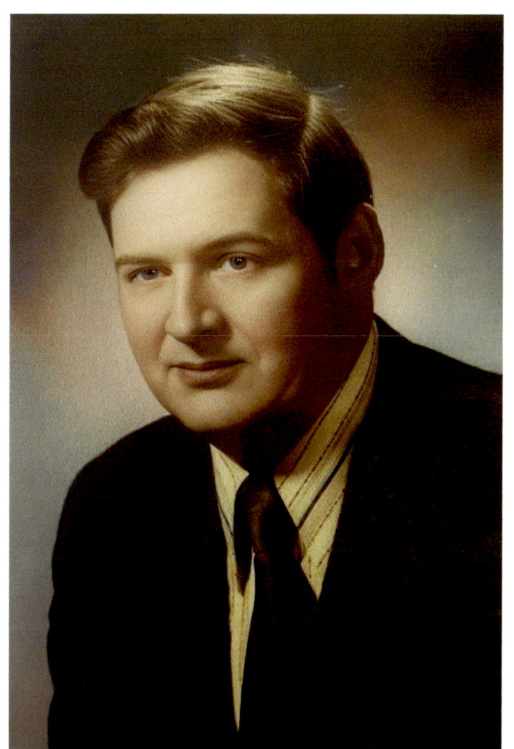 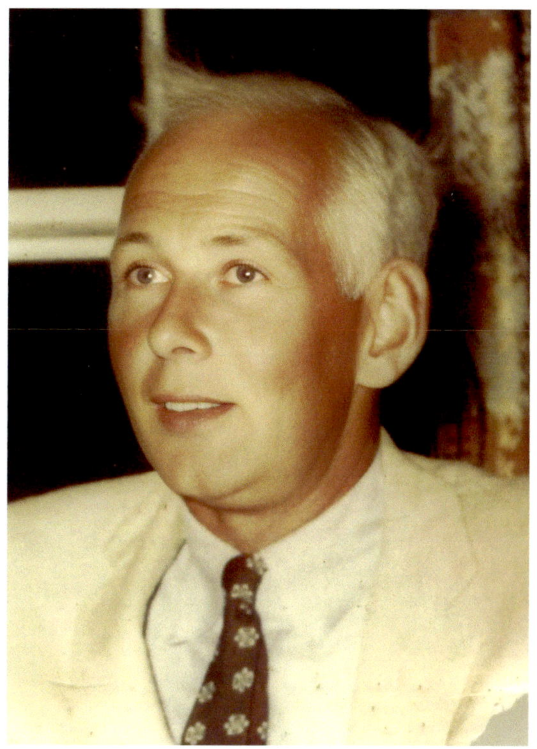

Above left: Richard K. Newcomb (1931–2004) attended Milton High School and served in the United States Navy. He was the City of Quincy purchasing agent and assistant director of Quincy City Hospital. He worked at his father's Newcomb Bakery, which had twenty-six bakeries in and around Boston and later owned a Mug 'N Muffin Restaurant in Quincy. In 1984, he would open Newcomb Farms Family Restaurants in Milton on Randolph Avenue, with others in Wollaston and Manomet. Newcomb Farms says that they "use the best ingredients and provide a great atmosphere" and their slogan is "It's never too late for breakfast, never too early for lunch!" During Thanksgiving, Newcomb donated so many fresh turkeys to shut-ins, the elderly, and homeless shelters that the Milton Kiwanis Club gave him its Special Community Recognition Award in 2000. (*Courtesy of Nancy Newcomb Frates*)

Above right: James Adams Roberts (1914–1959) graduated from Milton Academy and from Harvard. He worked in the insurance field before buying three businesses in Milton Village: Preston's, the Milton Exchange, and the Elastic Tip Company. He was the president of Preston's the Village Grocer at 75 Adams Street in Milton Village. From the 1800s to the 1960s, Preston's offered personal customer service combined with modern supermarket prices. Frank H. Hoadley was the manager, and the employees were Roy Carlson, Ted Czarnocki, and William Klehm. However, Roberts' passion was sports, hockey, tennis, and golf, both playing and watching. Having been a hockey star at Milton and Harvard and played semi-pro hockey after college, it was natural that he coached the Milton Academy hockey team in the 1950s. He raised much of the money for the construction of the first artificial rink at Milton Academy dedicated as the James A. Roberts Rink. (*Courtesy of Nancy Pattison Roberts*)

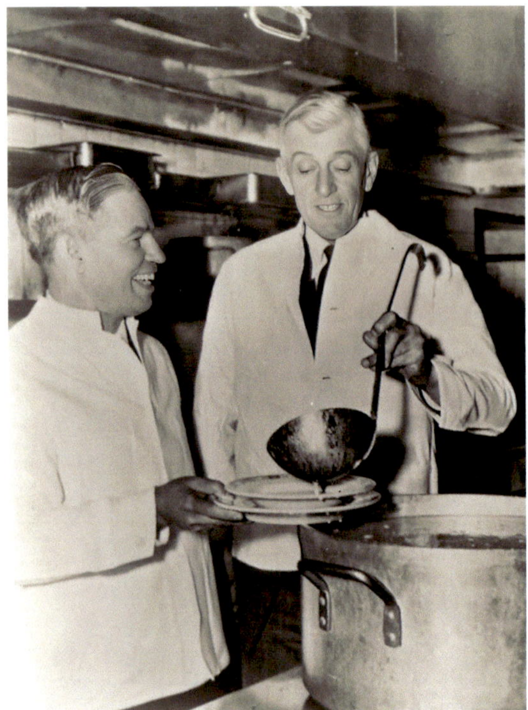 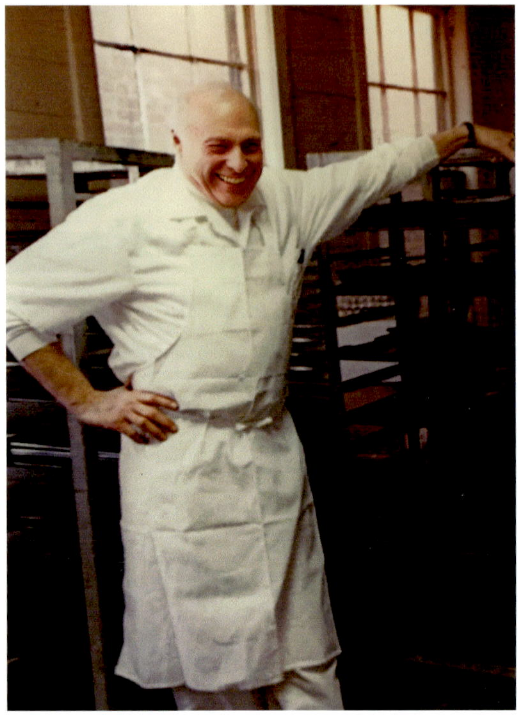

Above left: James Doulos (1906–1981) owned Jimmy's Harborside Restaurant, once located on Boston's Fish Pier. Born Demetrios Efstratiou Christodoulos in Mytilene, Greece, he called himself the "Little Greek," opening the Liberty Cafeteria in 1924 as a lunchroom, expanding it to seventeen stools and eventually building a restaurant that in 1955 was named Jimmy's Harborside Restaurant. Julia Child, the French chef from WGBH, said that she liked "Jimmy's very much. I like their shellfish and broiled swordfish" and the restaurant was awarded the esteemed *Holiday Magazine* "Award for Dining Distinction" for many years. One title bestowed on Doulos by a food magazine was the "Chowder King of the Nation." It stemmed from a request for chowder by his friend, Senator Leverett Saltonstall who is seen ladling a serving of chowder into a bowl held by Doulos. (*Author's collection*)

Above right: Eugene P. Pierotti (1929–2017) graduated from St. Sebastian's School and Villanova University. Pierotti bought Bent's and continued a tradition started in 1801 by Josiah Bent who baked "water crackers" or biscuits made of flour and water that would have shelf life during long sea voyages. The bakery sold their hardtack crackers used by troops during the American Civil War. In addition to the pilot, common, warming, and hardtack, Bent's sold a variety of baked goods, including their George and Martha Washington pies, both had powdered sugar on the top, the George with a cherry filling, and the Martha with a lemon filling. Pierotti landed a contract to supply cookies to the U.S. Navy, which continued through the Vietnam War; it also supplied the army, which stashed 55-gallon drums of Bent's long-keeping oatmeal raisin cookies along the route of the Alaskan Highway as emergency rations. Thus, Bent's was nicknamed "The Broken Cookie Factory" with the unbroken cookies being shipped to its wholesale customers; the broken cookies were sold to eager customers by the pound.

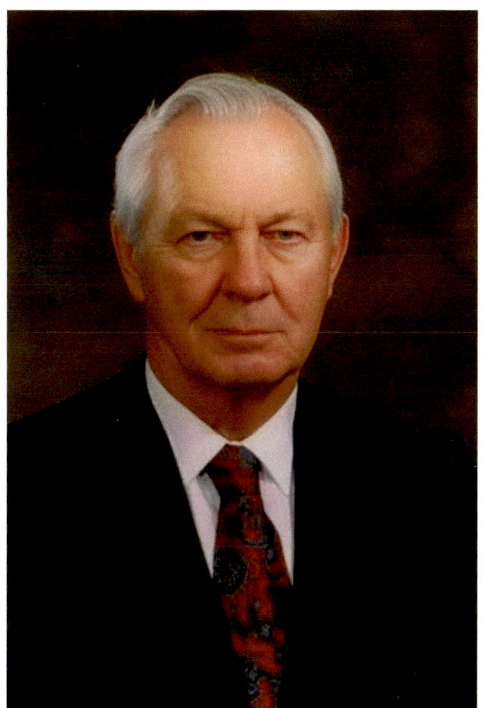 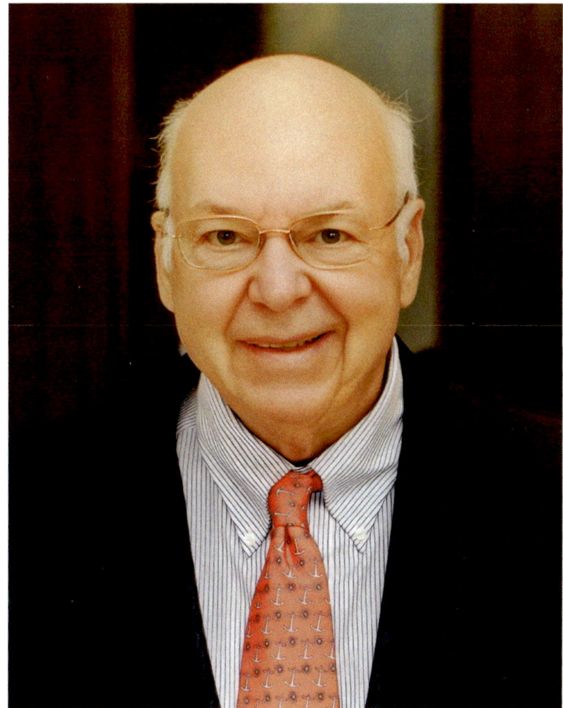

Above left: Jack Shaughnessy (1926–2013) attended Boston College High School and both Williams College and Tufts University. After serving in the U.S. Navy, he joined his brother, Herbert "Al" Shaughnessy, in their South Boston-based rapidly expanding crane, rigging, and aerial lift business known as Shaughnessy Crane Service, of which he became president. He served on many boards and commissions, especially of local Catholic causes; among these were the Board of Trustees of BC High, and Catholic Charities Boston, Labouré Center, South Boston; my Brother's Keeper, Easton; and both St. John's and Blessed John seminaries, in Brighton and Weston. The *Boston Pilot* said of him "He really did not like the limelight, even less did he like praise and acknowledgement for any of his many good works. And as many of those good works that were public and well known, there are many quieter and less known."

Above right: Donald J. Corey (1937–2020) owned Blanchard's Wine and Spirits, creating a chain of stores that offered a variety of libations for every palate. Blanchard's was originally established in 1838 by David W. Blanchard and John W. Farrar in Scollay Square Boston. In 1938, the company was purchased by Donald's father, John Corey, a visionary in the liquor industry. The family-owned company expanded with its own importing and distributing division as well as a distilled spirits and bottling plant in the South End of Boston. Donald Corey and his wife, Marcia, carried on the Blanchard tradition with successful and innovative retail liquor businesses in Jamaica Plain, West Roxbury, and Revere. Other Blanchard stores in Marshfield, Allston, and Brockton are individually family owned. The Blanchard tradition is now in the third generation. (*Courtesy of John David Corey*)

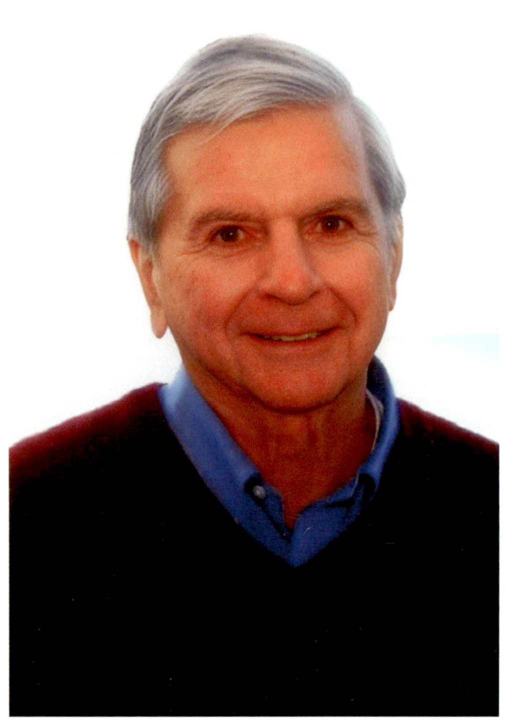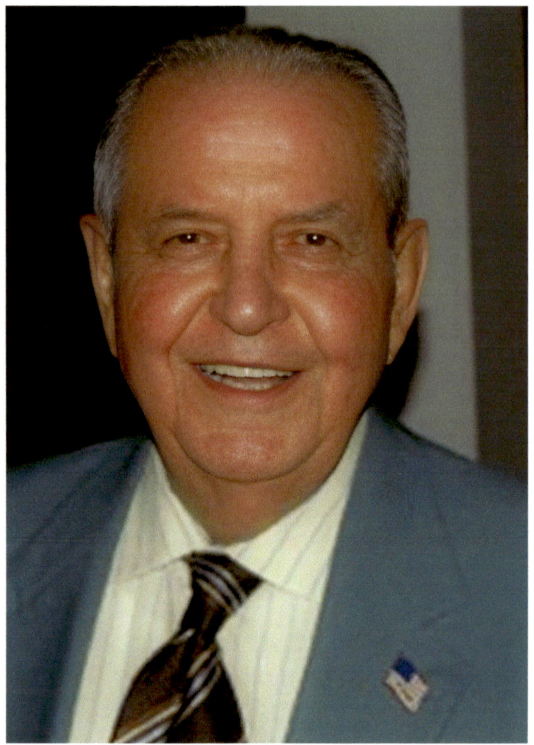

Above left: Robert Gannon White (1930–2022) attended Milton Academy, Georgetown University School of Foreign Service, and the Wharton School at the University of Pennsylvania. He was a U.S. Navy air intelligence officer in the Korean War, serving on the USS *Wasp* and the USS *Coral Sea* aircraft carriers. The White family ran the White Brothers Milk Company, delivering fresh milk to homes by Clydesdale horse. With his brothers, Allan and Donald White, in 1959 they transformed the family milk business into a regional ice cream and frozen food company called Hendrie's, which was founded in 1885 by Robert "Pop" Hendrie as Eliot Creamery. Hendrie's soon became known for its novelties such as the York Peppermint Patty Bar and the Minute Maid Orange Popsicle and producing private label ice cream for Stop and Shop and Benihana. The ice cream was sold throughout New England and enjoyed at Hendrie's Dairy Bar in Milton. White was president of Hendrie's and chairman of New England Frozen Foods cold storage in Southborough. Hendrie's was eventually purchased in 1989 by H. P. Hood Inc.

Above right: Alfred D. Thomas (1924–2015) served with the U.S. Army Medical Detachment 7th General Hospital, England, during "The Blitz." A well-respected undertaker, he started a funeral home in Mattapan Square and later moved to Granite Avenue in Milton. He was the founder and past president of the Massachusetts Horseman's Association, the former general manager of the Foxboro Raceway, a member of the United States Trotter's Assn., the New England Harness Horsemen's Assn., the Maine Harness Horsemen's Assn., and owned several prize-winning harness horses that raced throughout the country. Al Thomas was the sponsor of countless sports teams in the town of Milton and sponsor and biggest fan of the Al Thomas A's Yawkey League Baseball Team.

4
MILTON PHILANTHROPISTS

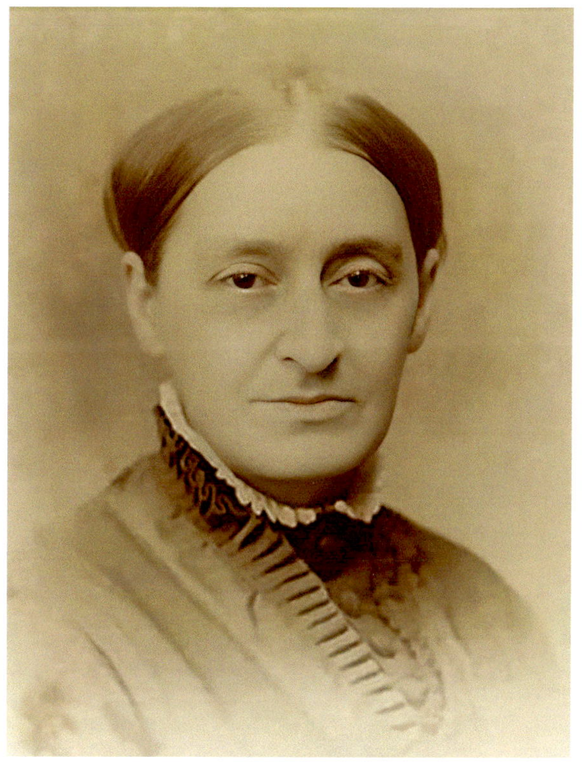

Elizabeth R. Swift (1820–1896), seen here, and her sister, Mary F. Swift (1828–1894), were founders of the Swift Charity Fund. A special act passed by the Massachusetts Legislature in 1898 formally established the Swift Charity as a nonprofit corporation. The charity was directed to either purchase a home or create a trust to assist needy and deserving women and children of Milton. The directors of this charity never established the "Swift Home" but instead have made grants to Milton residents and organizations benefiting Milton residents. Today, with other charity funds, it operates under the Milton Residents' Fund.

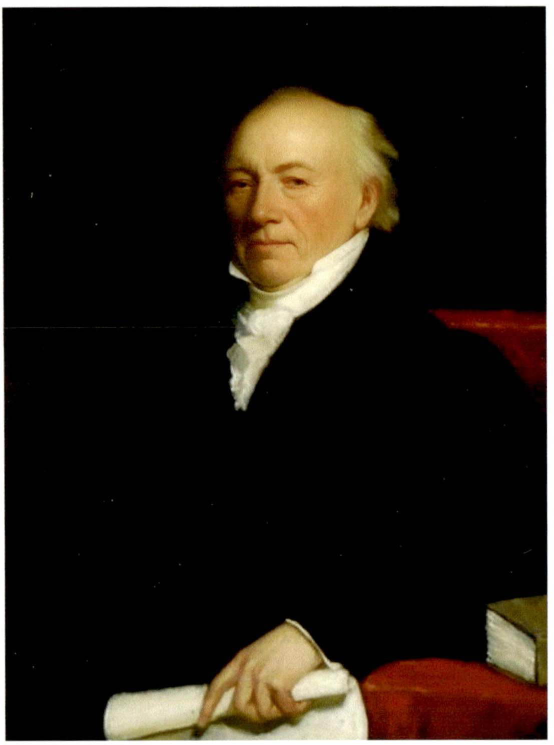

Edward Hutchinson Robbins (1758–1829) graduated from Harvard College in 1775. He became a lawyer, a delegate to the Massachusetts Constitutional Convention, and a state representative. After serving as speaker of the Massachusetts House of Representatives from 1793–1802, he became lieutenant governor of Massachusetts under Governor Caleb Strong from 1802–1806. In 1811, he was appointed judge of probate for Norfolk County. Robbins founded Milton Academy in 1798 as "a state-charted and partially subsidized institution" but the school only received its corporate charter in 1807.

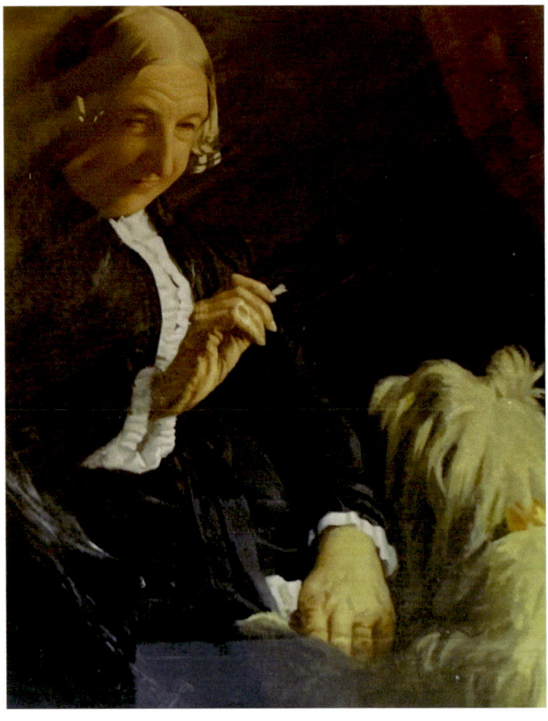

Mary Abbot Forbes Cunningham (1814–1904) was a great philanthropist. Upon her death, she stipulated in her will that her fortune should be held in trust "for the benefit of the inhabitants of Milton." Believing that open space for public recreation met this mission, the trustees purchased over 100 acres of land that had belonged to Mary's cousin, Edward Cunningham (1823–1889). When Cunningham Park opened in 1905, it offered Milton residents two tennis courts, two bowling alleys, and a gym remodeled out of a barn. Just like today, the meadow in the back was flooded in winter for skating and for many years both the High School and Milton Academy played their hockey games there. (*Courtesy of Cunningham Park*)

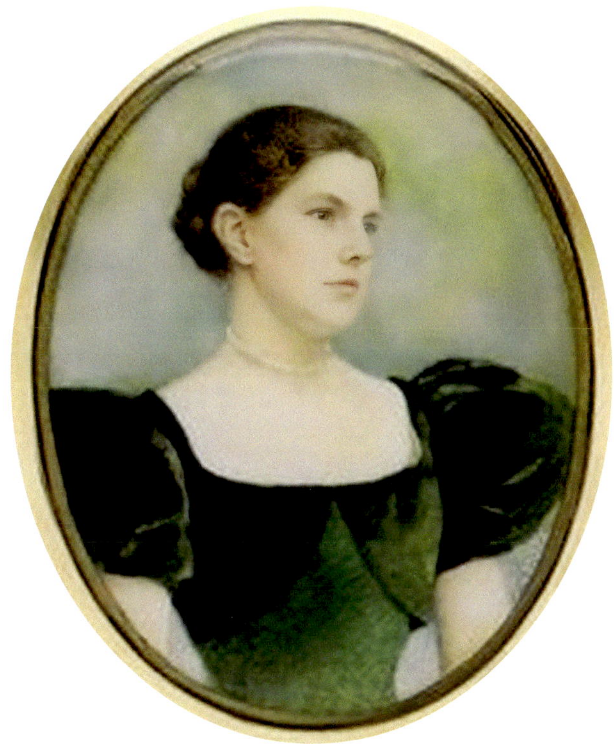

Annie Lawrence Rotch Lamb (1857–1950) commissioned and financed the Church of the Holy Spirit in Mattapan Square to be built in memory of her father, Benjamin Smith Rotch of Milton, which was designed by her brother, Arthur Rotch. Rotch used the outcroppings of puddingstone on the lot to create a stone and wood church set in a rustic setting which was sensitive to the topography of the site. Arthur Rotch of the Boston architectural firm of Rotch and Tilden created an urbane and sophisticated design, and it was not just an architecturally important place of worship, but also served as a place of worship for Episcopalians in the area. In the 1970s, the Lamb Estate, known as Pine Tree Brook, became H.O.M.E., Inc. (*Collection Museum of Fine Arts*)

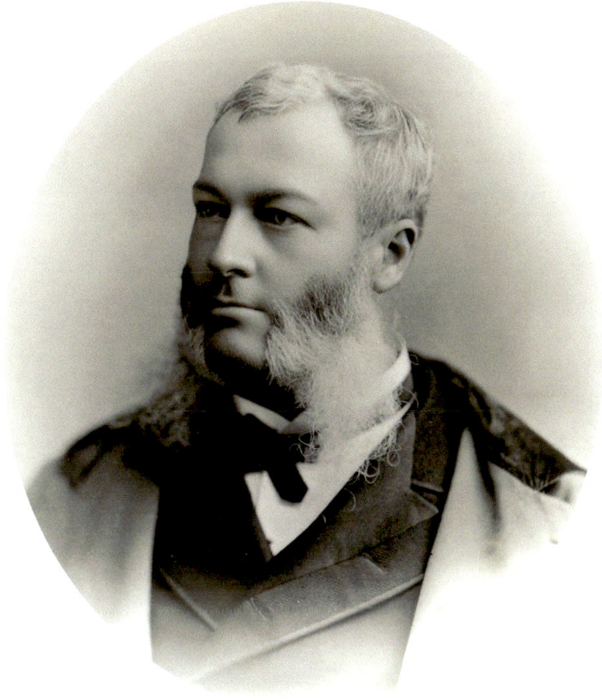

Oliver White Peabody (1834–1896) trained as a clerk in the office of John E. Thayer & Brother. During the Civil War, he served as lieutenant colonel in the 45th Massachusetts Infantry Regiment from 1862–1863. Following the war, he returned to John E. Thayer & Brother until he and his brother, Francis, along with Henry P. Kidder, founded the investment firm of Kidder, Peabody & Co. He and his wife, Mary Lothrop Peabody (1837–1910), were instrumental in the building of All Saints Church in Peabody Square Dorchester. At their suggestion Ralph Adams Cram was asked to propose a design for the new church which was consecrated in 1895. (*Author's collection*)

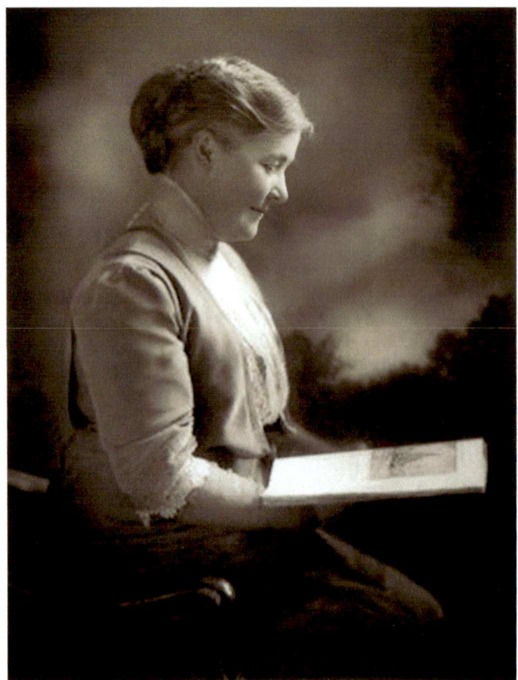 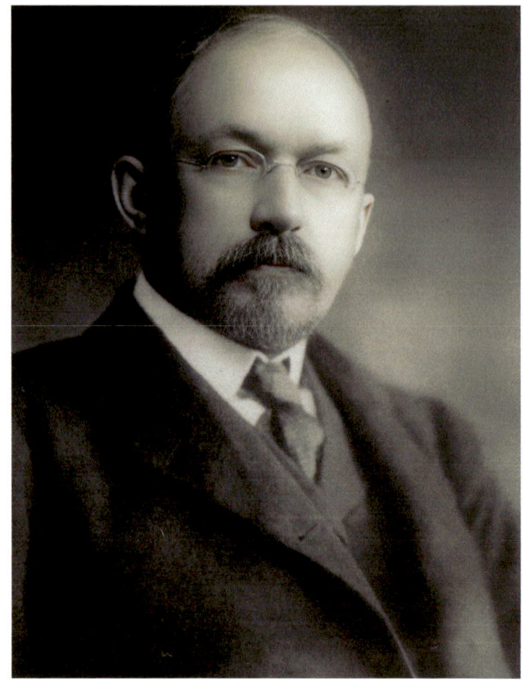

Above left: Rose Dabney Forbes (1864–1947) was a noted activist and participated in many peace organizations including the American Peace Society, the Massachusetts Peace Society, the Massachusetts branch of the Woman's Peace Party, and the World Peace Foundation. She was also a supporter and member of the Boston League of Women Voters, the Milton Women's Club, and the Women's National Committee for Law Enforcement. A native of Faial Island, Azores, Portugal, she was the daughter of Samuel Wyllys Dabney who served as United States consul in Horta from 1872–1892; she was the second wife of John Malcolm Forbes.

Above right: Nathaniel Thayer Kidder (1860–1938) graduated from Harvard College and later attended the Bussey Institute. He was a noted philanthropist and Milton's first tree warden. Son of Henry Purkitt Kidder, co-founder of Kidder, Peabody & Company, he served as president of the trustees of the Milton Public Library, the Museum of Fine Arts and the Massachusetts General Hospital and was largely responsible for providing the funds to build the Milton Public Library, designed by Shepley, Rutan and Coolidge and built in 1904, as well as the Kidder Branch and the East Milton Branch of the Milton Public Library. He was a leading member of the Massachusetts Horticultural Society serving as president for three years, a member of the New England Botanical Club, and a benefactor of the Gray Herbarium of Harvard University

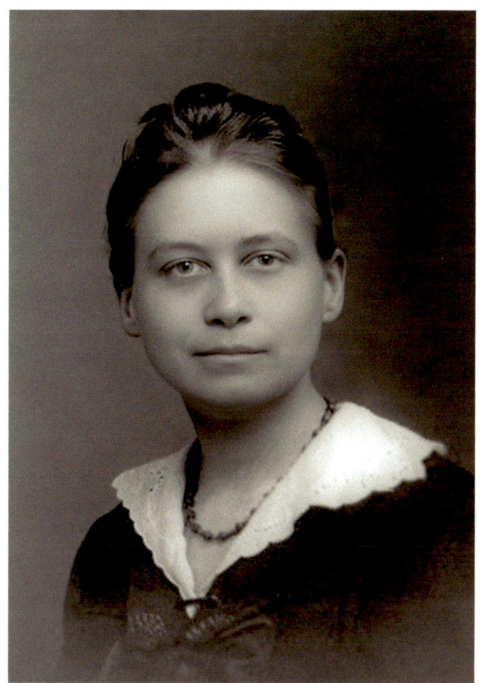 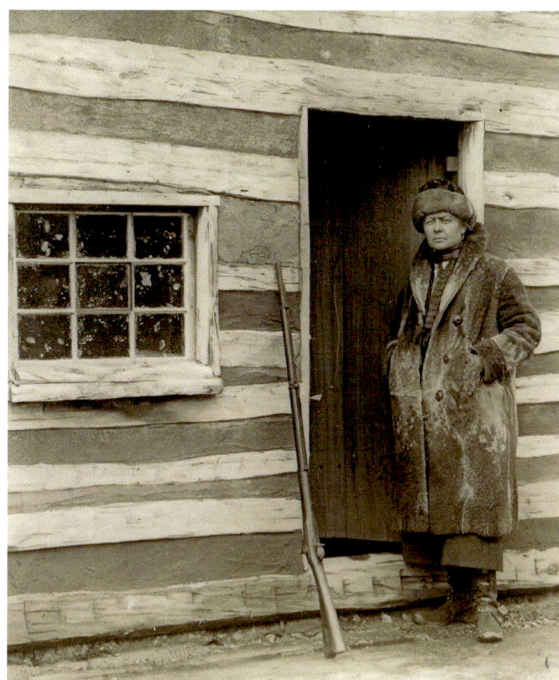

Above left: Dr. Anna Quincy Churchill (1884–1971) graduated from Smith College, earned a master's degree in biology at Radcliffe College, studied at the Boston School of Gymnastics, and completed her medical degree at Tufts University School of Medicine. She was the first woman to serve on the faculty of Tufts University School of Medicine and School of Dental Medicine from 1918–1954. Churchill established scholarships for biology undergraduate students, which were in memory of her parents, and made personal loans to Tufts Dental School students in need. She was awarded the Distinguished Service Key by Tufts in 1955.

Above right: Mary Bowditch Forbes (1878–1962) was a horse and dog enthusiast, admirer of Abraham Lincoln, amateur poet, political conservative, anti-pacifist, and anti-suffrage lobbyist. She took her admiration of Abraham Lincoln to a new height when she had Thomas Murdock built a replica of Lincoln's log cabin birthplace on the family's estate in Milton. It was open to the public, especially on Lincoln's birthday when Baker's Cocoa was served for those waiting in the cold to see the cabin, and filled with Lincoln-related photographs, prints, furniture, and mementos. (*Courtesy of Forbes House Museum*)

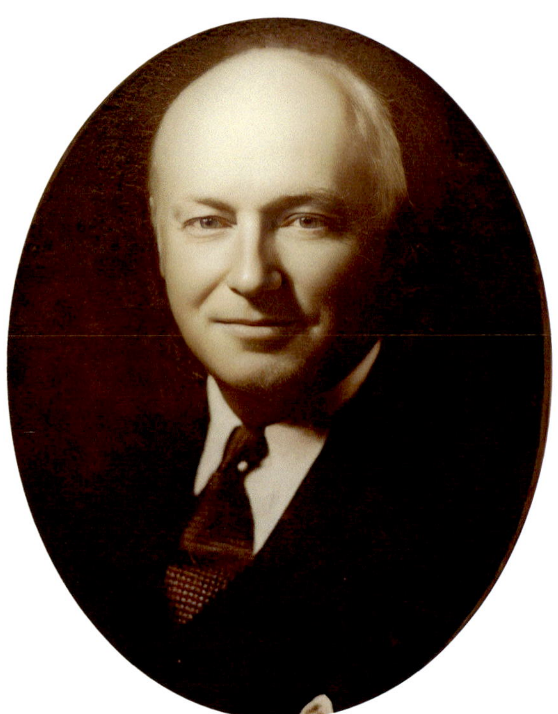 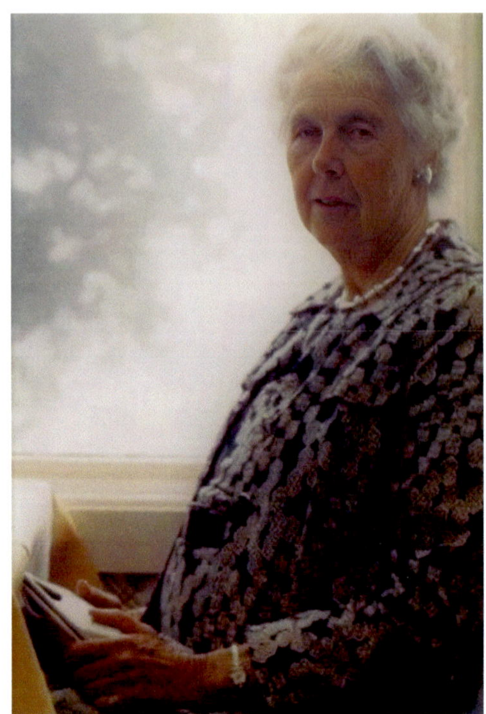

Above left: Harold Whitworth Pierce (1885–1958) was a partner at Tucker, Anthony & R. L. Day, a Boston investment banking and brokerage firm. He established upon his death the Harold Whitworth Pierce Charitable Trust, which offers grants primarily for projects that will produce long-range benefits. Grants are made for specific programs, for seed money, and for capital projects and have enriched many worthy causes throughout the Boston area. (*Courtesy of The Country Club, Fred Waterman*)

Above right: Rosamond Lamb (1898–1989) was educated at the Winsor School. She was described as a modest, gentle, and an unassuming lady. She and her sister, Aimée Lamb, were great philanthropists to many Boston institutions. The donation of family portraits, paintings, and acquired art to the Museum of Fine Arts was legendary, as well as Lamb's bequest to the Boston Athenaeum for a book fund. The Lamb family archives were donated to the Massachusetts Historical Society and are testimony to their foresight for preservation. In Milton, the sisters donated in 1974 a Powder House, which was located on their property, to the Town of Milton in honor of the Bicentennial. Their everlasting legacy was when in 1978 they sold 33 acres of land to H.O.M.E. Inc. with 14 acres set aside for conservation purposes. The Town of Milton accepted conservation restrictions imposed by the Lamb sisters and agreed to by the Warrant Committee. The remaining 32 acres, located on the south side of Canton Avenue, were sold to Richard C. Fitzgerald of Milton for the Quisset Brook Condominiums.

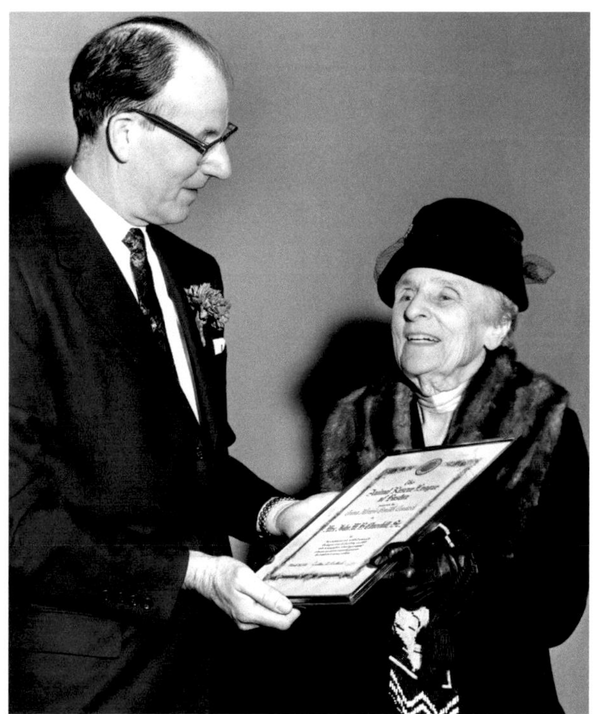 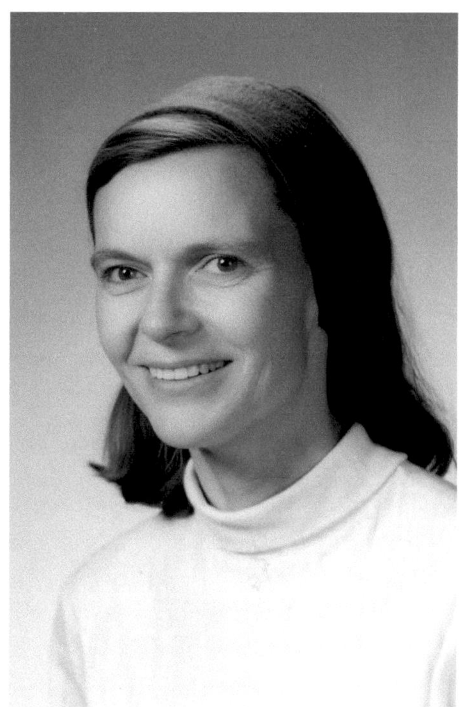

Above left: Anne Allen Ely Churchill (1898–1983) was an incorporator, longtime trustee, honorary vice-president, and supporter of the Animal Rescue League. Founded by Anna Clapp Harris Smith in 1899 as a rescue mission for every kind of animal, the league's motto was "kindness uplifts the world," the cornerstone upon which league was built. Seen here, she was presented with the Smith Award in 1962 by Carlton Buttrick, president of the League as the sole remaining member of the founding board. (*Author's collection*)

Above right: Marjorie Shaw Jeffries (1928–2019) attended Bryn Mawr College and received an MA in music composition from Connecticut College. She played an active role in the town of Milton as a Trustee of the Milton Public Library, was a driving force behind the library renovation, was a longtime leader of the library book group, and was a Milton town meeting member for over thirty years. Forthright and opinionated, she was an advocate for land conservation, environmental causes, women's equality, and preservation of the Fowl Meadow conservation area on the Neponset River, and the Neponset River Bike Path. (*Courtesy of Peter Jeffries*)

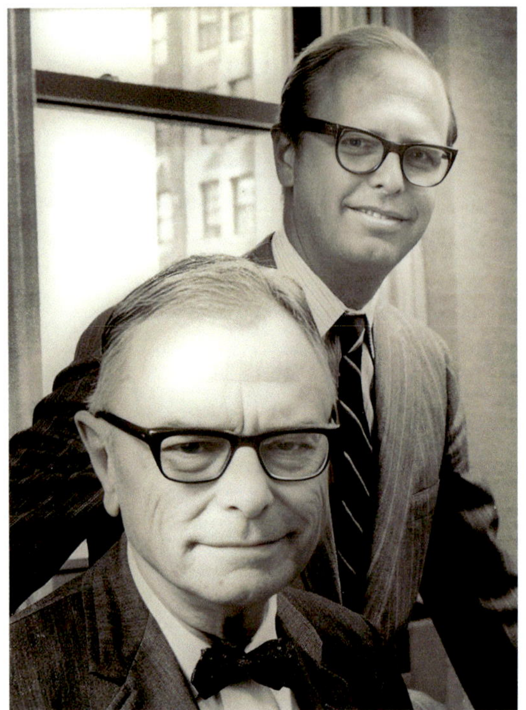 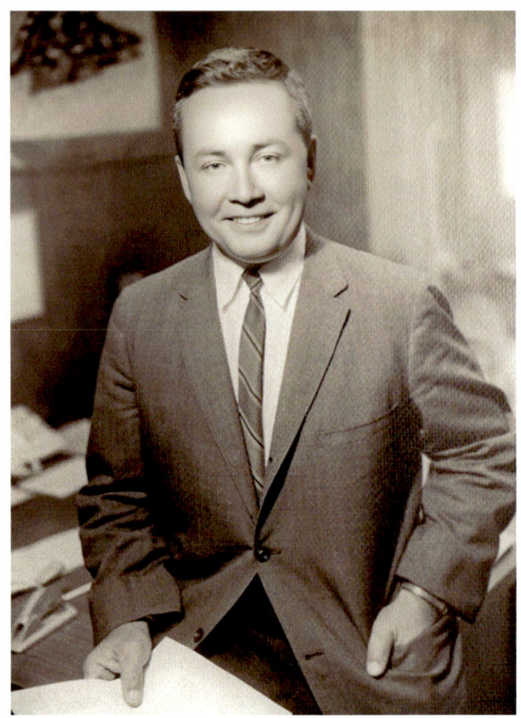

Above left: Edward Crosby Johnson II (1898–1994), seated, and his son, Edward Crosby Johnson III (1930–2022), represented many decades of investment acumen. Incorporated in 1930, during the Great Depression, the "Fidelity Fund" was the only fund approved by John C. Hull in his term in office as securities director for Massachusetts because of widespread bank failures. In 1943, Johnson II was elected president and director of the Fidelity Fund. Johnson III served as chairman of the board and the chief executive officer of FMR Corporation, the parent company of Fidelity Investments and in 1977 was elected CEO of FMR Corporation. (*Author's collection*)

Above right: Duncan Forbes Will (1920–1983) was part of the second generation of Wills to be born in Milton graduated from Milton High and the Franklin Institute in Boston. He was president and treasurer of the A. A. Will Sand and Gravel Corporation and Pine Street Realty Corp., a real estate development business. He was a member of the Massachusetts Charitable Mechanics Association and the Canton Association of Industries. As a tribute to Mr. Will's work ethic and honesty, this business organization raised the funds necessary to build the first senior center in Canton. The D. Forbes Will Senior Center was located on the ground floor of the Hemenway School (which was converted to senior housing by the Canton Housing Authority in 1980) and it served the senior community for three decades before moving to its current location, the former Knights of Columbus Hall. (*Courtesy of Anthony Will*)

5

$\mathcal{D}$ISTINGUISHED $\mathcal{M}$ILTONIANS

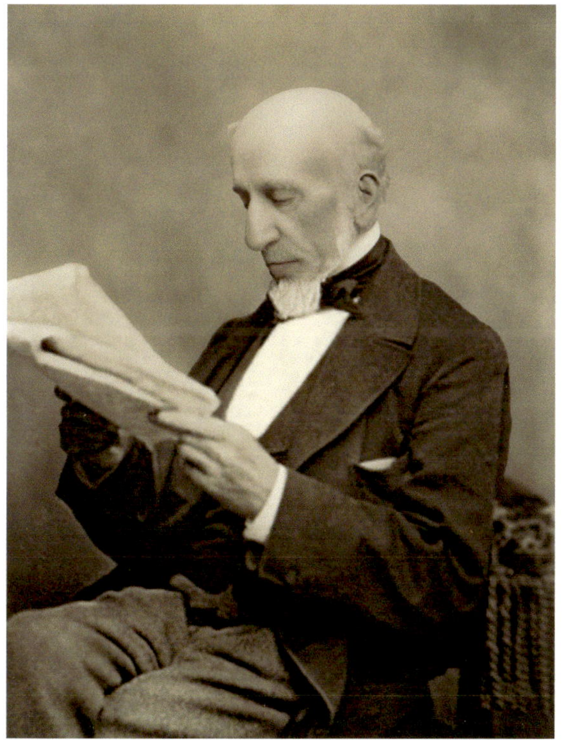

John Murray Forbes (1813–1898) made his fortune in the American house of Russell &
Company in China where he was a partner. He was chairman of the National Republican
committee in Abraham Lincoln's administration, and developed the Chicago, Burlington,
and Quincy to the position of the largest and strongest road system of the American West.
He was a director of the Chicago, Burlington, and Quincy Railroad for more than forty
years and during most of that time he was chairman of the board of directors, and for
several years he was president of the company.

59

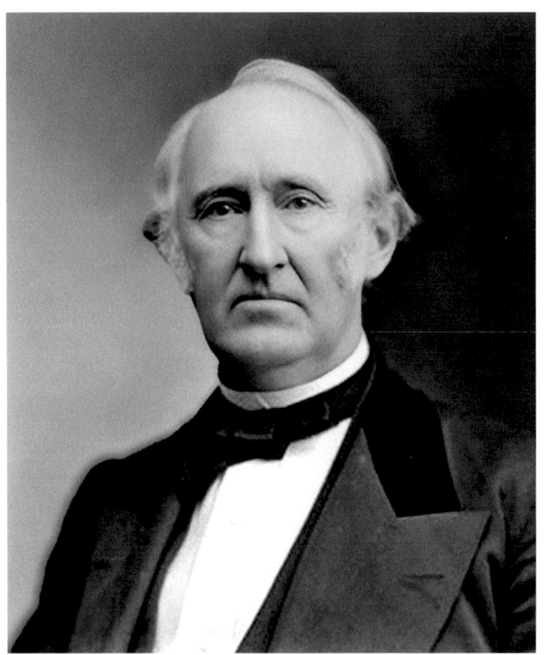 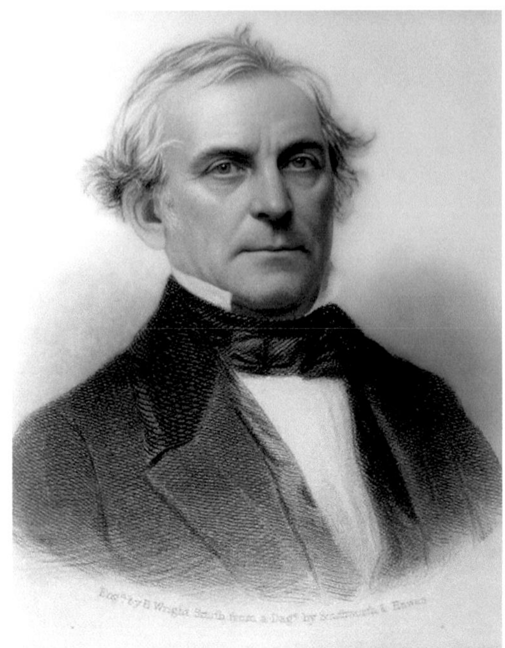

Above left: Wendell Phillips (1811–1884) graduated from Harvard in 1831 and from Harvard Law School in 1833. He was admitted to the Massachusetts state bar in 1834 and opened a law practice in Boston. Phillips was socially conscious and concerned about social issues, such as abolitionism, women's rights, universal suffrage, temperance, and the labor movement. Phillips was originally buried at the Granary Burying Ground in Boston, but his remains were moved to the Milton Cemetery in 1886 and buried with his wife, Ann Terry Greene Phillips (1813–1886.) (*Author's collection*)

Above right: Gideon French Thayer (1793–1864) was the founder in 1828 of Chauncy Hall School in Boston, serving as headmaster from 1828–1855. A private preparatory school, Chauncy Hall was located on Chauncy Place and educated the children of wealthy Bostonians for careers in business, and later prepared students to attend Harvard, MIT, and other prestigious colleges. Chauncy Hall was known for its many innovations in education, including using literature for reading lessons, and implementing a department system to recognize teachers who were "gifted and accomplished in different directions." The school thrived in the mid-1800s under Thayer, who was also an advocate for better education nationwide. Chauncy Hall became a model for many new institutions. Thayer was the author of *Letters to a Young Teacher*, published in 1859. Today the school is known as Chapel Hill-Chauncy Hall School in Waltham.

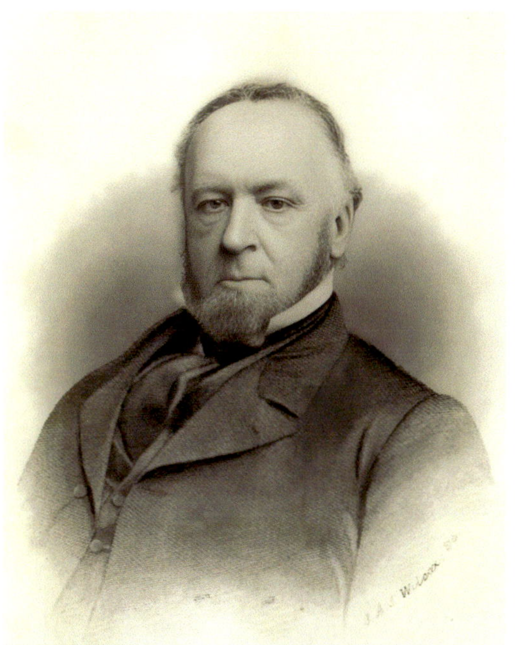 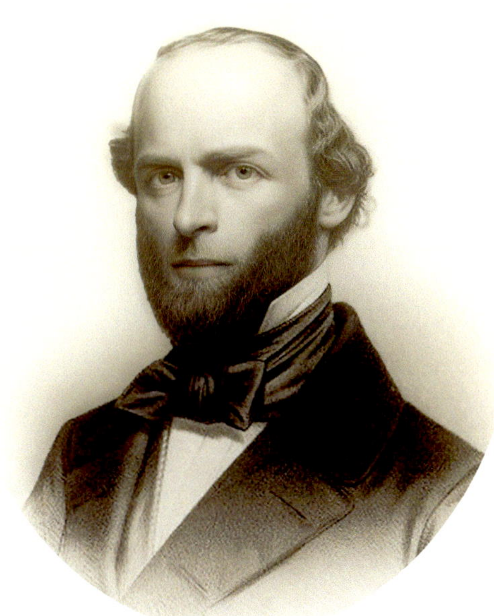

Above left: James Murray Robbins (1796–1885) attended Milton Academy and served as supercargo to the West Indies under James and Thomas Handyside Parkins. He was named U.S. Consul-General at Hamburg, Germany, in 1841, and conducted business in Europe. He was also a real estate speculator, buying 20,000 acres at Passamaquoddy, now in Maine, which he sold in 1834. He had a large estate on Brush Hill in Milton, where he lived for fifty years. He served as justice of the peace, first president of Milton Academy as well as the Milton Public Library. He also served as a Massachusetts state representative and senator. Dr. Teele said of him "He was always approachable to those needing advice and assistance, and his wise counsel and helpful words and deeds have lifted many a heavy burden."

Above right: Henry J. Gardner (1818–1892) was a dry goods merchant who served on the Boston Common Council between 1850 and 1854. He became a member of the anti-immigrant "Know Nothing" Party in 1854 and was the candidate of the Know-Nothing movement and was elected governor as part of the sweeping victory of Know-Nothing candidates in the Massachusetts elections of 1854, losing only in the town of Phillipston. In line with the nativist and anti-Catholic politics of the Know-Nothing movement, Gardner proposed an amendment to the Massachusetts state constitution banning appropriations of tax funds to Catholic schools, which was passed by the state legislature and ratified after it was approved by referendum.

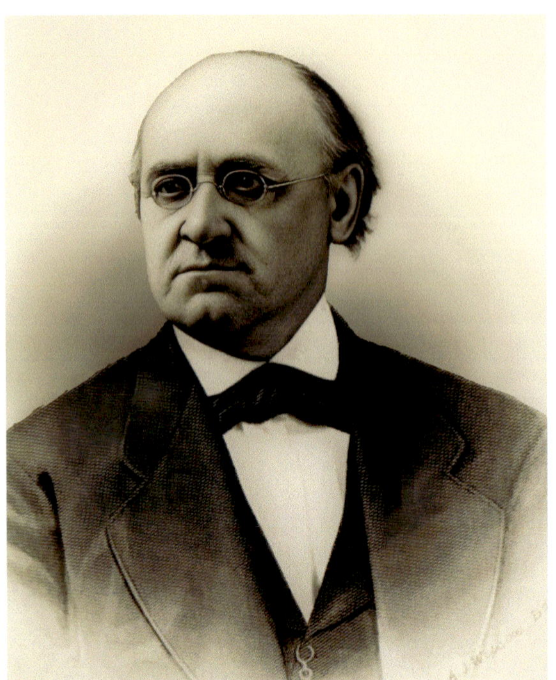 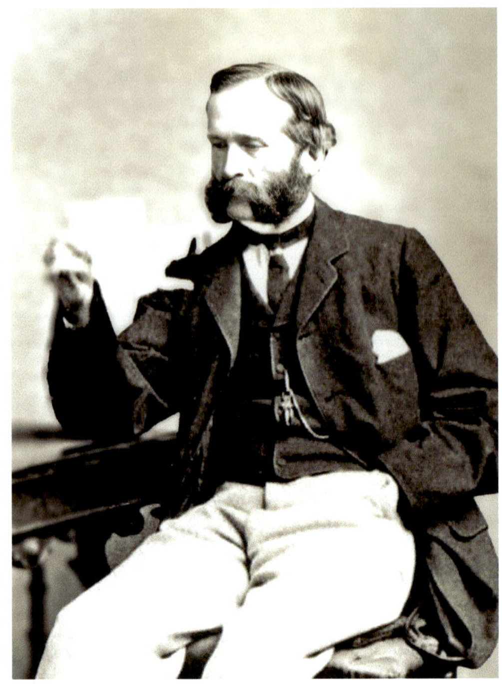

Above left: Nathaniel Foster Safford (1815–1891) prepared for college at the Latin Grammar School in Salem and graduated from Dartmouth College. He studied law with Hon. Asahel Huntington, of Salem, and commenced practice in Dorchester and Milton Village. In the early years of his professional life, he functioned as a magistrate, and as master in chancery, also exercising jurisdiction under the operation of insolvent laws. In 1848 when Abraham Lincoln campaigned for Zachary Taylor, who was running for the presidency, he stayed at Safford's house in Lower Mills. He was a representative to the General Court from the town of Dorchester in 1850 and 1851.

Above right: Edward Cunningham (1823–1889) was a partner in Russell & Company and made a fortune in the China Trade. He retired to Milton in 1857 and built a large house that was set on an extensive estate. Cunningham was killed in 1889 on his property by a trespasser. His widow continued to live in the mansion until 1905 when a "Dower house" was built on the site of the present Community Gardens. The estate, except for about 15 acres along Cedar Road, was sold to the Trustees of the Mary Abbot Cunningham Trust (she was a cousin of Edward Cunningham) and is today known as "Cunningham Park." The Milton Hospital and Convalescent Home operated in the former Cunningham mansion for almost fifty years. (*Courtesy of Edith Cunningham Crocker*)

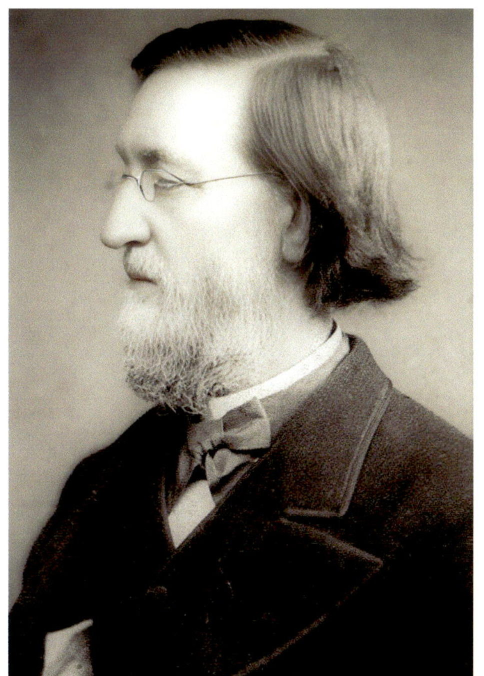 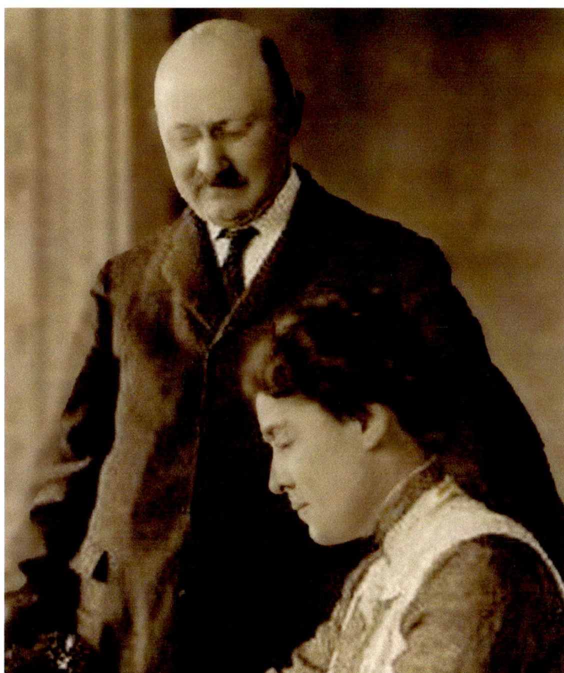

Above left: Rev. J. Peter Lesley (1819–1903) graduated from the University of Pennsylvania where he was trained for the ministry. He entered Princeton Theological Seminary and graduated from the seminary in 1844, being licensed to preach by the presbytery of Philadelphia. He worked for two years for the American Tract Society. He accepted the pastorate of the Milton Congregational Church and remained there until 1851, when, his views having become unitarian, he abandoned the ministry, returned to Philadelphia, and entered practice as a consulting geologist. His wife was Susan Inches Lyman Lesley (1823–1904), the author of *Letters of James Murray, Loyalist,* and *Recollections of my mother, Mrs. Anne Jean Lyman.* Rev. Lesley was elected to the American Philosophical Society in 1856 and served as was president of the American Association for the Advancement of Science.

Above right: Henry Winchester Cunningham (1860–1930) attended Roxbury Latin School and Harvard College. Cunningham was able to retire at twenty-eight when the family's business, the Continental Sugar Refinery, was sold to a larger refining concern. He then devoted himself to history, genealogy, and philanthropy; he was the author of *Brief Sketch of the Old Milton Church: Its Ministers and Meeting Houses, 1678–1928.* He was involved in many organizations including the New England Historic Genealogical Society and the Colonial Society of Massachusetts. His wife, Mary May Cunningham (1863–1929), inherited the Wakefield Estate in Milton after her mother's death in 1901; her parents were Isaac Davenport and Mary Vose Hayward. At his death, Cunningham left $100,000 to Milton Hospital in memory of his late wife. A separate gift of $10,000 was given contingent upon the hospital erecting a bronze tablet in memory of Mrs. Cunningham. The memorial tablet can be seen at the Highland Street entrance.

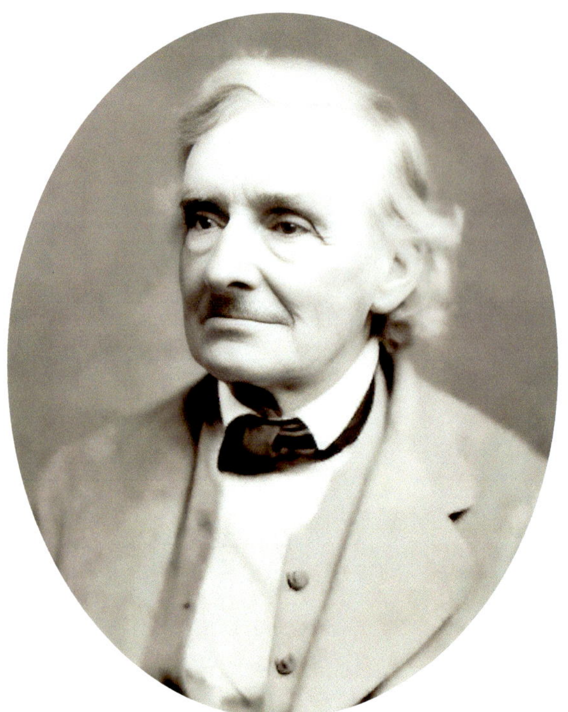

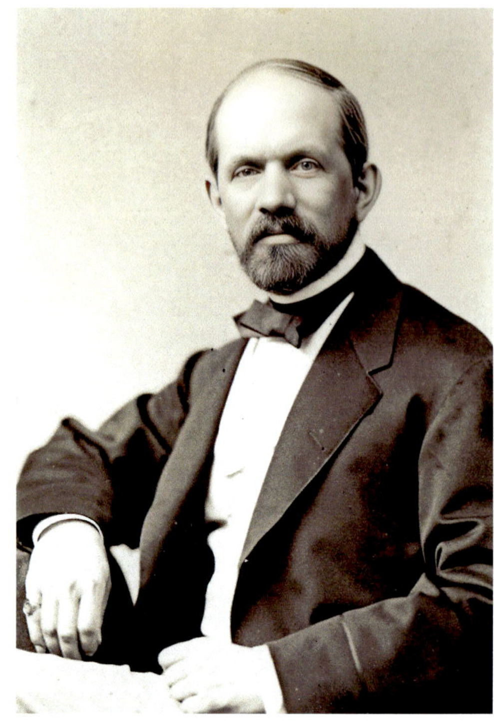

Above left: Edmund James Baker (1804–1890) was a cartographer by trade, and one of his early surveys was that of the towns of Dorchester and Milton in 1831. Baker was the grandson of both Daniel Vose and Dr. James Baker, who founded the Baker Chocolate Company. For several years he was a resident of Milton, and in 1837 was the representative of that town to the General Court. From 1838–1842, he was the postmaster in Milton. Subsequently he moved to Dorchester Lower Mills and built a large house at the corner of Washington and Richmond Streets. He was one of the founders of the Dorchester Antiquarian and Historical Society, and from 1873 to the time of his death was its president. (*Courtesy of Marion White Woodbridge*)

Above right: Henry Purkitt Kidder (1823–1886) graduated from Boston English High School. In 1838, he became a clerk in a grocery store, and shortly thereafter he became a clerk in the office of Coolidge & Haskell. In 1847, he joined J. E. Thayer & Brother, where he learned banking. In 1865, Kidder, Francis H. Peabody, and Oliver Peabody, all of whom had worked as clerks at Thayer & Brother, established Kidder, Peabody & Company. In 1882, Kidder donated an Italian marble sculpture of an angel, purportedly by Giovanni Benzoni, for the Milton Cemetery's "ornamental lot." This prompted the trustees to make their decision that the lot would now be called "the charitable lot" and be available for those in need, with the marble angel prominently placed in the center of the lot.

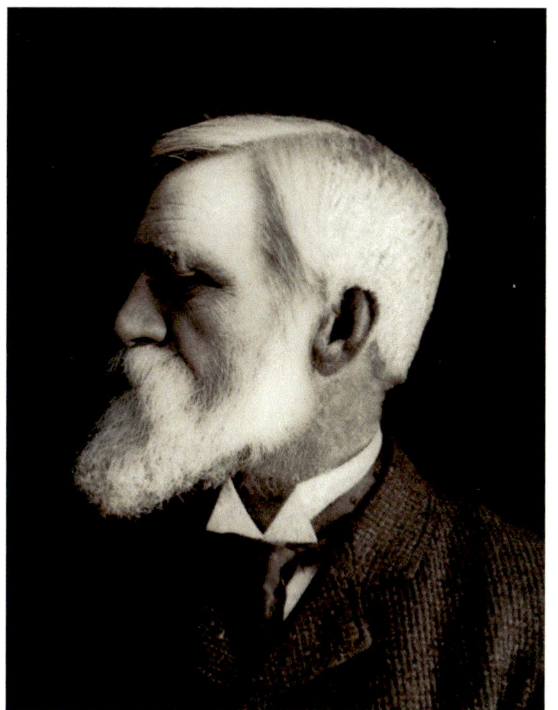 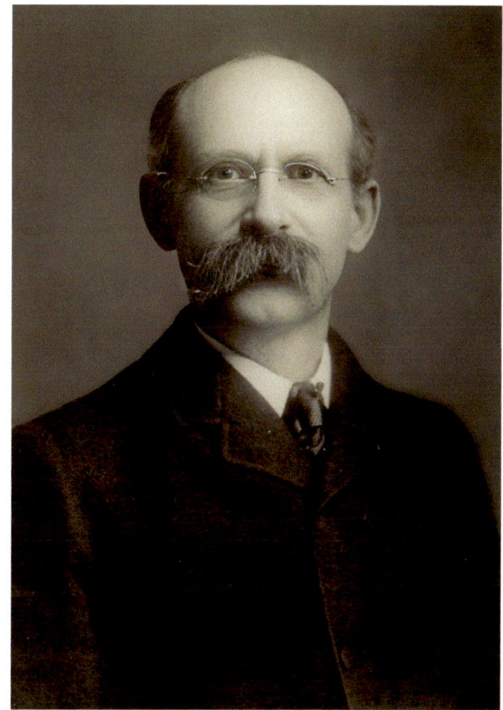

Above left: John Boies Tileston (1834–1898) attended Milton Academy and Boston Latin School and graduated from Harvard. He was in partnership with Thomas Mayo Brewer in the firm of Brewer and Tileston Company, well-known printers and booksellers, and in the 1870s would annually print the *Old Farmer's Almanac*, not changing the format and content and continuing the heavy focus on farming and weather predictions. Tileston was the son of Edmund Pitt Tileston, who with Mark Hollingsworth had the Tileston and Hollingsworth Paper Company in Mattapan. At the death of his brother, Francis Lowell Tileston, his interest in the company of Tileston and Hollingsworth passed to John Boies Tileston, who was also a partner of the Boston publishing firm Brewer and Tileston. His wife was Mary Wilder Foote Tileston (1843–1934), a prolific author of the spiritual and inspirational works *Daily Strength for Daily Needs* and *Joy and Strength* and of genealogical materials and memoirs.

Above right: Orrin Alvin Andrews (1848–1916) was a teacher and later principal at the East Milton Grammar School, serving from 1871–1916. The cow pasture of James Smith, who lived on Granite Place in East Milton, had been given to the town of Milton to remain as open land. In 1940, Andrews Playground was opened on Belcher Circle and has offered recreation for generations of Miltonians. Today there is a basketball court, two Little League baseball diamonds, a pickleball court, playground, soccer, softball field, and three tennis courts. One person sang the park's praises saying "Really great park and playground for kids of all ages. Clean, new, and plenty of benches and parking. It's popular, even in the winter. It's next to a basketball court, where you'll find kids riding bikes and scooters. There's also a big field for running around."

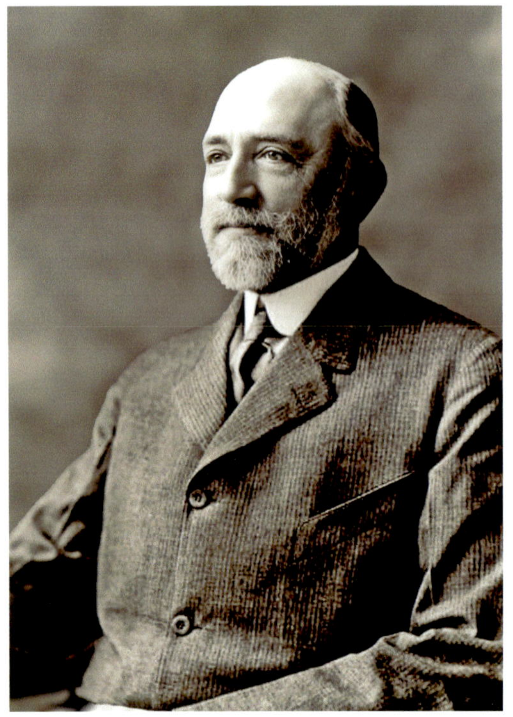

Dr. Matthew Vassar Pierce (1855–1937) attended Boston Latin School and was a graduate of Harvard College and the Harvard Medical School. Dr. Pierce continued his medical studies at clinics and hospitals in Berlin, Heidelberg, and Vienna. In 1903, he founded the Milton Convalescent Home, which was the forerunner of the Milton Hospital, of which he served as chief of staff for three decades. He was said to have carried "comfort, skilled care, unfailing kindness, sympathy and understanding to practically every member of town, at one time or another." He was perceived as unassuming, reassuring, and diligent in his ministering to the ill in town, and he was said to have become "a much loved doctor here until his death." (*Courtesy Frances Pierce Field*)

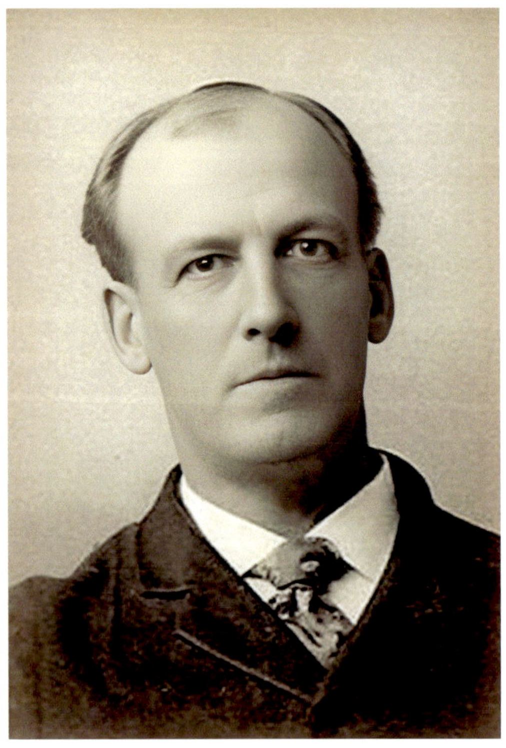

Dr. John Malcolm Forbes (1901–1941) graduated from Harvard in 1923. After graduation, he traveled to Africa with a relative, Gerrit Forbes. J. Malcolm Forbes pursued post-graduate studies at Columbia and was an assistant professor of psychology at Rollins College for four years, beginning in 1928. He received his Ph.D. in psychiatry from the University of London, and then worked for the Harvard Psychological Clinic and taught at Simmons College. Forbes was interested in welfare work and active in the Judge Baker Foundation until his death in 1941.

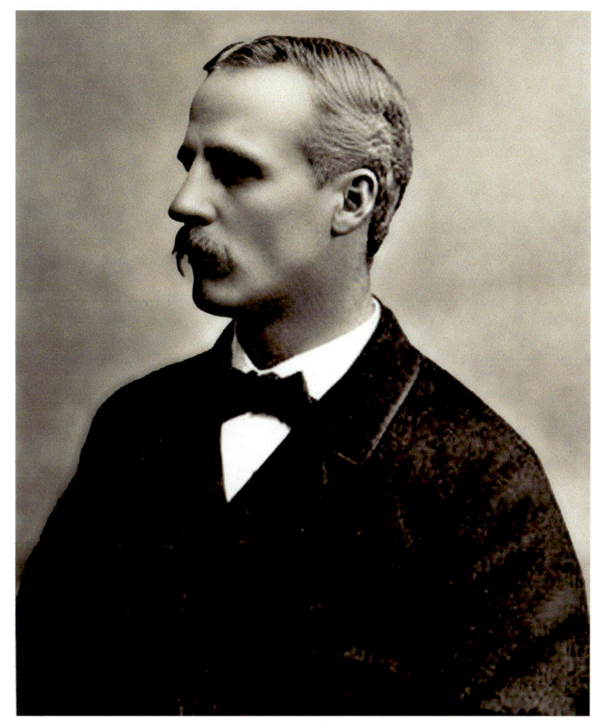

William Hathaway Forbes (1840–1897) was fitted for college by E. S. Dixwell and H. L. Patten and attended Harvard. He served in the Civil War as second lieutenant, Company E, First Massachusetts Cavalry, and later the Army of the Potomac. He was promoted to first lieutenant in 1862, and in 1863, to captain. He was made major of the Third Battalion, Second Massachusetts Cavalry, 1863. He was honorably discharged in 1865. In the 1870s, he was approached by Gardiner Greene Hubbard and Thomas Sanders to invest in their Bell Telephone Company. Not only did Forbes invest, but he also encouraged some of his wealthy acquaintances to do so as well. Subsequently, Forbes served as the president of the Bell Telephone Company from 1879–1887.

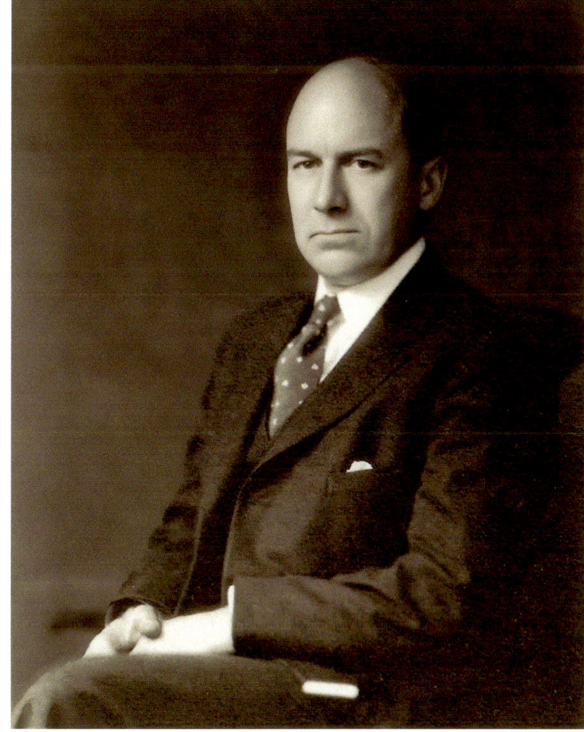

Stanley Cunningham (1856–1909) attended the Boston Latin School and graduated from Harvard. He was a clerk in Boston and then, for several years, did business as a cotton broker. About 1883, he became a member of the firm of Barnes & Cunningham, stockbrokers. This firm dissolved partnership in 1895. In 1897, Cunningham became treasurer of the Electric Tool Company of New York with offices at 78 Devonshire Street, Boston; and from 1900–1902, he was a note broker at the same place. Later he took the superintendency of the Safe Deposit Vaults of the Old Colony Trust Company in Boston.

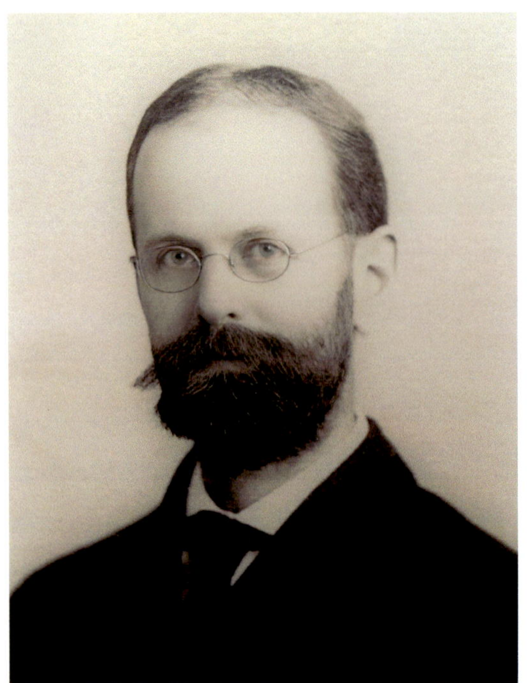 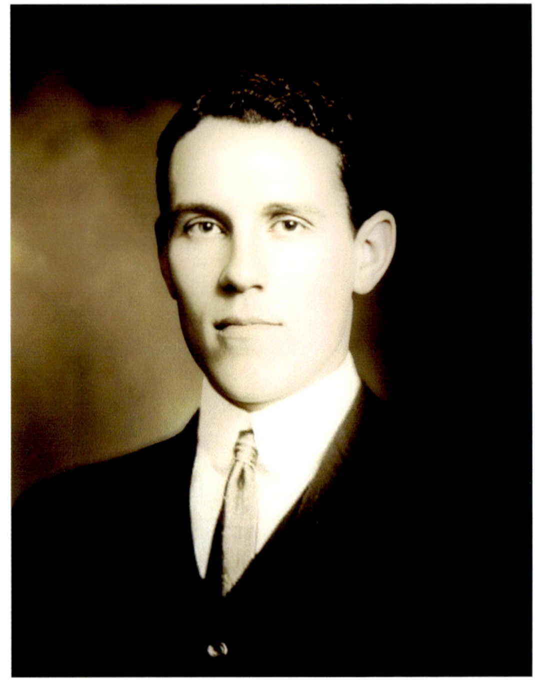

Above left: Samuel Johnson (1860–1932) attended Dartmouth. He was the president of C. F. Hovey and Co., a department store on Summer Street in Boston. Hovey's was started in 1833 by Charles Fox Hovey, an importer and jobber of dry goods. Hovey was an innovator and marked goods with a one-price system, the adoption of early closing hours, profit-sharing for employees, a credit system, and utilizing monthly bills, were just some of the now-standard practices first appearing in Hovey's. Johnson, the progenitor of the Fidelity Johnsons served as president until 1926, and later his son, Edward Crosby Johnson, served as president before he founded Fidelity. Jordan Marsh bought Hovey's in 1925, though it retained the Hovey name until 1947.

Above right: John White Hallowell (1878–1927) graduated from Harvard. He was a financier and manager of the Stone and Webster securities department. At the outbreak of World War I, he became chairman of the New England Committee for Supplementary Rations for Belgian Children. He served as an assistant to Herbert Hoover in the U.S. Food Administration in Belgium and other parts of Europe and later became assistant to Secretary of the Interior Franklin K. Lane. He was appointed to the U.S. Council of National Defenses Emergency Employment Committee for Soldiers and Sailors. He served on the boards of Children's Hospital and the Middlesex School in Concord, was treasurer of the *Harvard Alumni Bulletin*, treasurer of the Harvard Alumni Association, a member of the Harvard Fund Council, president of the Harvard Associated Clubs, and the Board of Overseers at Harvard University from 1914–1925.

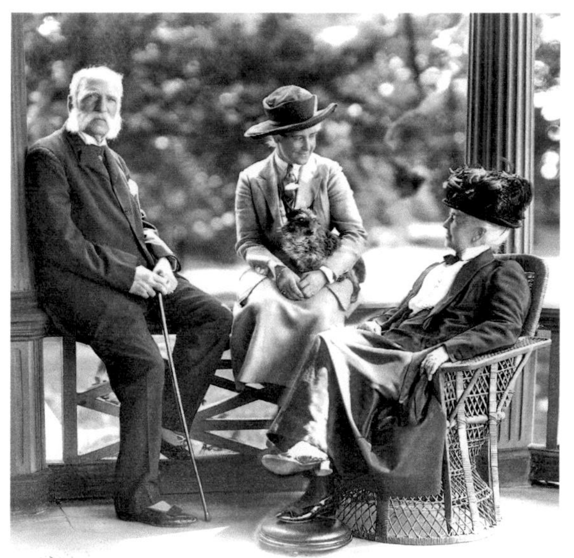 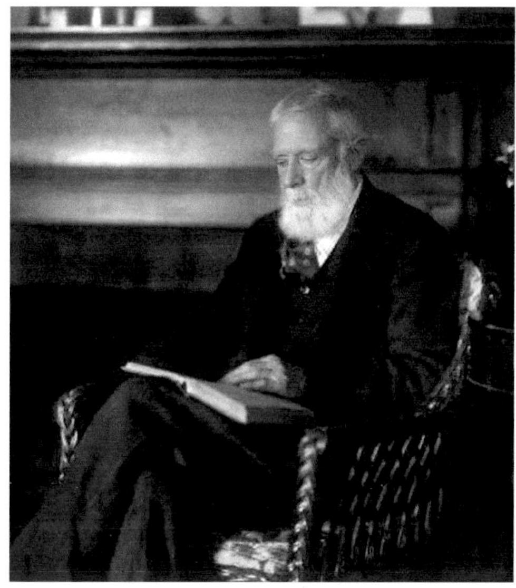

Above left: James Murray Forbes (1845–1937) seen with his wife, Alice Bowditch Forbes (1848–1929), and their daughter, Mary Bowditch Forbes, was a prosperous China trade merchant who went to China in 1863 for Russell & Company. Starting as a clerk with Russell & Company, Forbes advanced rapidly in the family firm and, in 1871, returned to the United States a very wealthy man. In 1897, a year after the death of Henry Lillie Pierce, Forbes headed a syndicate of Boston capitalists and businessmen which purchased the ten thousand shares of stock in Walter Baker & Company, Ltd. The Forbes Syndicate implemented a new cooling system and air conditioning, which allowed the production of chocolate in warm weather, and systematically purchased electric-and gasoline-powered delivery trucks to replace the horse-drawn wagons. Advertising and marketing of the chocolate and cocoa were expanded, with full-page color advertisements in nationwide magazines, leading to widespread use of Baker's Chocolate and Cocoa. (*Courtesy of Forbes House Museum*)

Above right: Silas Pinckney Holbrook (1833–1920) was a partner of Thomas Bailey Fox in the firm of Holbrook & Fox, a noted real estate and land auction company in Boston. The firm was founded in 1870 and was known for its influence and reliability in the real estate market, and it was said "being residents of Boston, the partners are successful appraisers, and they hold the position of reliable auctioneers of real estate." The members of the firm comprised S. Pinckney Holbrook, Charles B. Fox, and William Channing Clapp, and they buy, sell, and exchange lands, lots, and houses, loan money on bond and mortgage, effect insurance in reliable companies, and take the entire charge of estates. "Their books contain descriptions of some of the choicest property in Boston and vicinity, and their business has been developed to success by honorable methods. A specialty is made of Dorchester property." Holbrook was a world traveler, and he wrote *Sketches, by a Traveler.* (*Collection of Boston Athenaeum*)

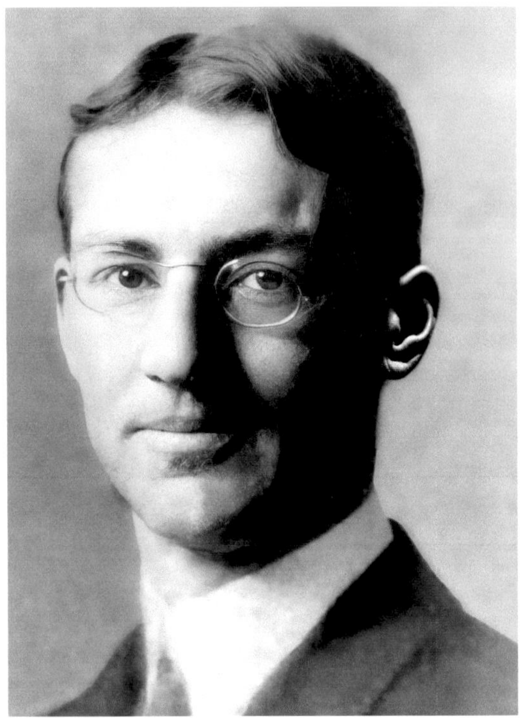

Kenneth Grant Tremayne Webster (1871–1942) was graduated from Dalhousie University, with an undergraduate degree from Harvard University, followed by a master's and doctorate there, after which he was immediately offered a faculty position at the institution. He was a scholar of medieval literature who devoted his academic career to the study of medieval romances, castles, and the art of war. However, though a prominent literary scholar, his claim to fame was the moving of the seventeenth-century Barnard Capen House from Codman Square in Dorchester to his estate on Hillside Street in Milton. He also saved the Ross-Thompson House in Shelburne, Nova Scotia, which he bought to save it from demolition, and which is now a museum. (*Courtesy of Harvard University Archives*)

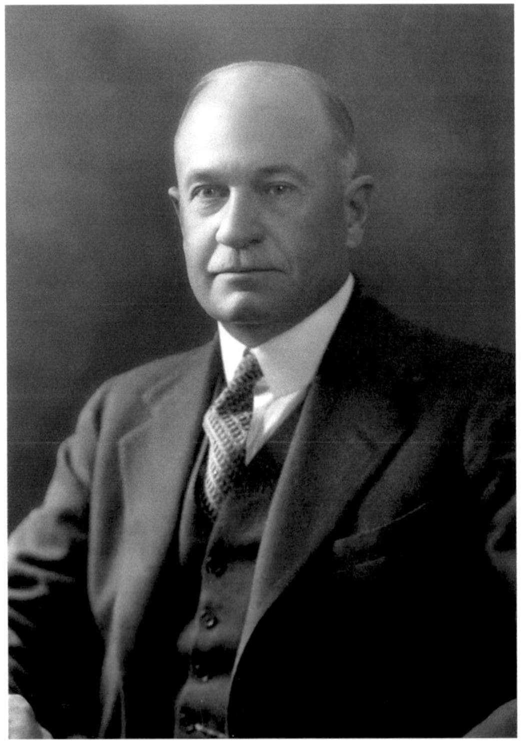

Charles Woodbury Whitter (1866–1949) was educated at the Prince School and Boston English High School. In 1900, he founded C. W. Whitter & Brother, a real estate firm in Boston he started with his brother, Albert Ropes Whittier. Their father, Albert Rufus Whittier, had been a very successful Boston real estate dealer in the late nineteenth century. Whittier was in real estate for sixty years and served as a trustee of the Boston Five Cents Savings Bank and a member of the Boston Real Estate advisory council. (*Author's collection*)

Patrick T. Maguire (1867–1910) was a well-known stone cutter. He was in business with James F. O'Heron (1859–1897) in the firm of Maguire & O' Heron and their quarry was at the northeast foot of the Blue Hills about 800 feet southwest of the last quarry off Pleasant Street in Milton. Cutting and polishing was done in sheds in East Milton, now the location of the Milton Marketplace. Maguire & O'Heron was commissioned to erect the Pilgrim Monument in Provincetown, agreeing to build the monument upon the existing foundation and using granite from the quarries of John L. Goss of Stonington, Maine. Ornamental work was done in sheds in East Milton and when completed the monument was the tallest all-granite structure in the United States.

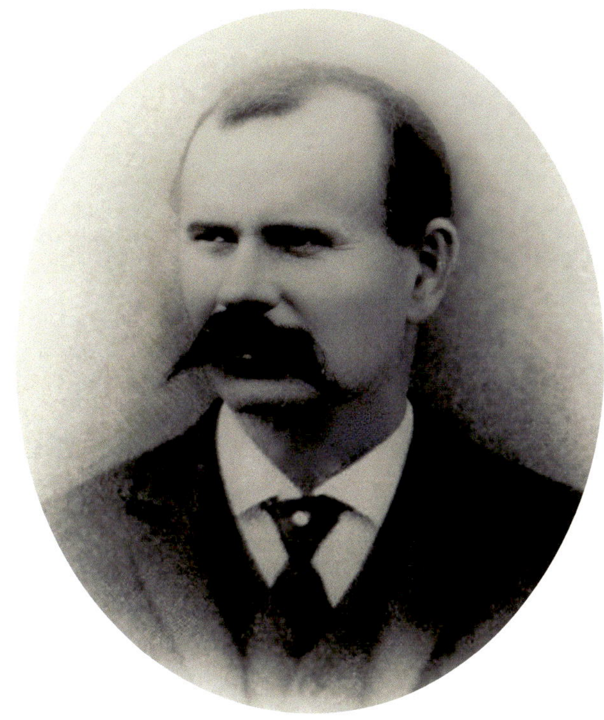

Markham Winslow Stackpole (1873–1949) was a member of the Milton Academy faculty from 1923–1938 and was later minister and historian of Milton Academy. In a history of the motto *Dare to be True*, former Milton faculty member Markham W. Stackpole wrote: "For us, the meaning of those words 'Dare to be true' goes beyond truthfulness in intent, speech, and action, vastly important as that is, and includes the three great principles of courage, truthfulness, and loyalty." The Milton Public Library annually awards a scholarship to library pages from the Stackpole Scholarship Fund. (*Courtesy of Milton Academy Archives*)

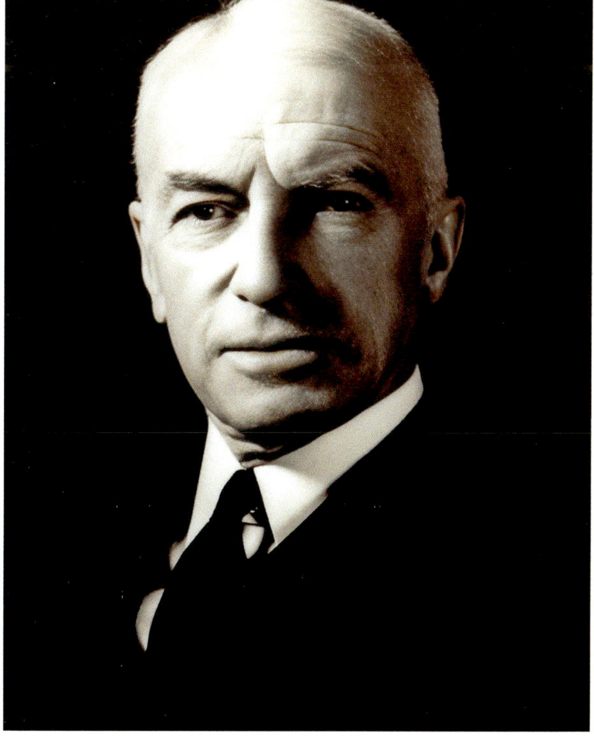

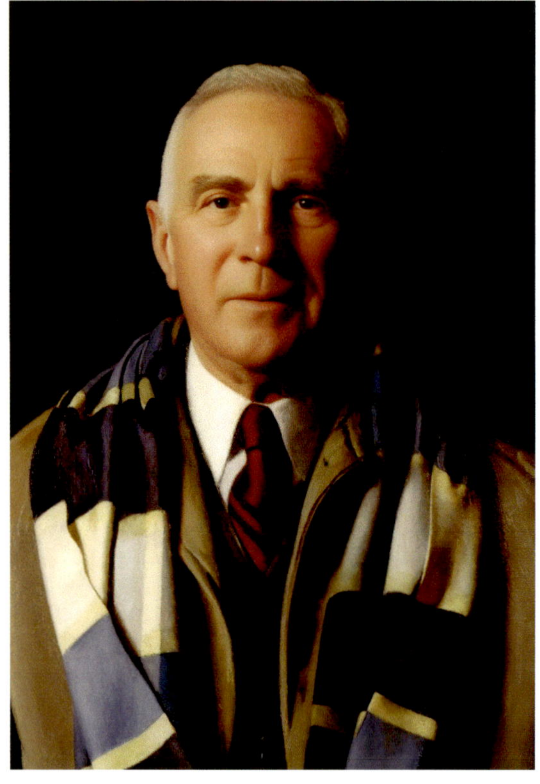

Arthur Stanwood Pier (1874–1966) attended St. Paul's School and Harvard and worked on the editorial staff at the *Youth's Companion*. He also edited the *Harvard Graduates' Magazine*, and at that time taught English courses at both Harvard and Radcliffe. He also taught English at St. Paul's School. He was the author of *Bits of Milton History*, *The Story of Harvard*, *The Pedagogues: A Story of The Harvard Summer School*, the *History of St. Paul's School*, and *Forbes: Telephone Pioneer*, and two dozen more. His headstone states "One of America's finest writers a brilliant gallant man with countless friends." His portrait is by R. H. Ives Gammell. (*Collection of Boston Athenaeum*)

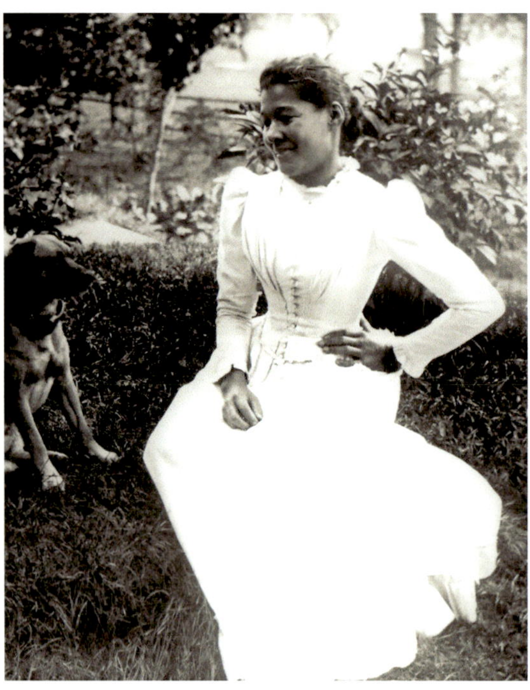

Mary Crowd Chappelle (1862–1933) was the daughter of George and Mary Emeline Crowd, descendants of the Punkapog. During her lifetime, she took great interest in the concerns of the tribe and was their memory keeper. She could recount family names which, within her memory, had died out such as the Bancroft and Moho. She suggested that there was some mixture between the Punkapog and the Narragansett because she thought there was a Narragansett family named Bancroft at one time at Indian Lane. In 1896, she married George C. Chappelle, a member of the Mi'kmaq Tribe from Prince Edward Island. They lived at 970 Canton Avenue, in the house her father Daniel Crowd, a stonemason, bought in 1860 when he moved from Canton to "Blue Hill Village" near the corner of Canton Avenue and Harland Street in Milton. Mary Chapelle continued to live there, working as a dressmaker until her death.

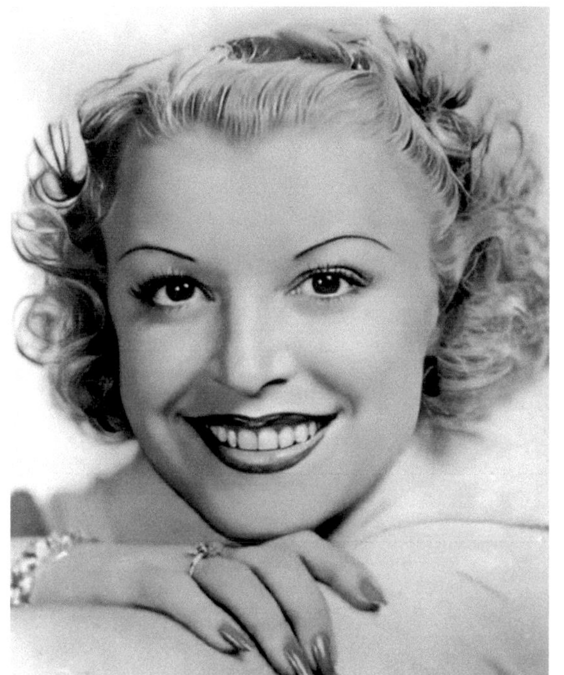 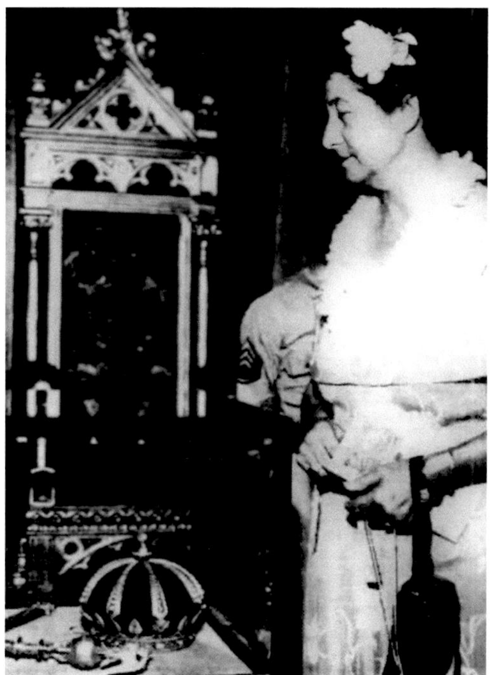

Above left: Collette Lyons Hearst (1908–1986) attended the New England Conservatory of Music studying voice. She was a performer in stage and musical comedy revues such as Weston & Lyons with Bob Weston. A versatile performer in plays such as Al Jolson's *Hold onto Your Hats*, she would appear in occasional films such as *Three Texas Steers, Frisco Sal, Blondie's Big Deal, Three Texas Steers,* and *Return to Peyton Place.* In the 1950s, she acted in television, starring in *The Life and Legend of Wyatt Earp.* She was married to George "Fanny" Randolph Hearst, living at his estate San Simeon in California; he was the eldest son of the late publisher William Randolph Hearst and served as vice-president of the Hearst publishing empire. She was the fifth of his six wives.

Above right: Lorna Kahilipuaokalani Iaukea Watson (1885–1972) was born in Hawaii of *kaukau ali'i* rank, meaning lower-ranking chiefs in service to the royal family. Her middle name "Kahilipuaokalani" was bestowed upon her by King Kalakaua of Hawaii. Her parents, Charlotte Kahaloipua Hanks and Curtis Piehu Iaukea, were not official members of the royal family, though they descended from King Kamehameha I and King Keku'iapoiwa II. She was the wife of Edward Bowditch Watson (1880–1959). She was co-author with Curtis P. Iaukea of *By Royal Command: The Official Life and Personal Reminiscences of Colonel Curtis Pi Ehu Iaukea at the Court of Hawaii's Rulers.* The book is about her father, a noted career diplomat of the Kingdom of Hawaii. Seen here she is admiring the Hawaiian royal regalia at the Iolani Palace in Honolulu. (*Courtesy of Iolani Palace, Hawaii, Zita Cup Choy*)

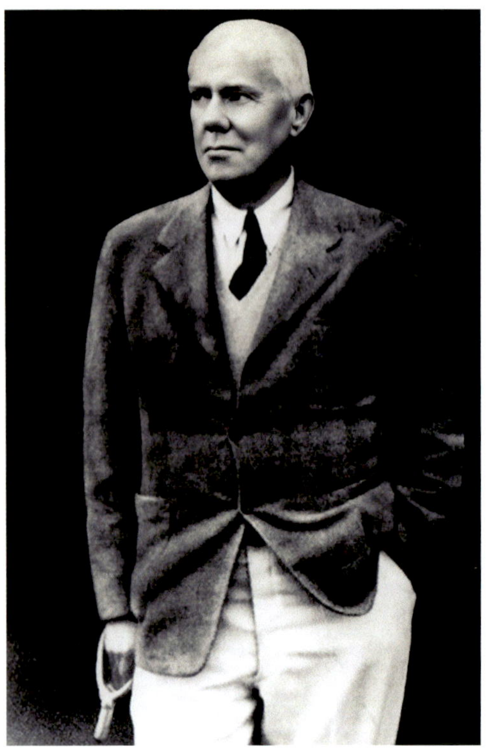 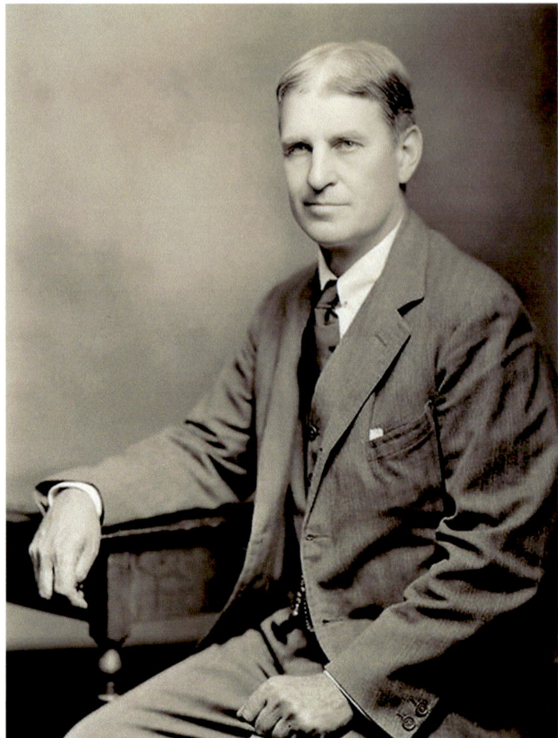

Above left: Robert Wheaton Rivers (1882–1945) was graduated from Harvard, after which he was head of the English Department at Noble and Greenough School. He was to become headmaster of the Rivers School in 1915 for fourteen years; he led the school through its early years, ensuring that the goal of open-air education was followed. Rivers and two other teachers led classes, and in the afternoon, the students played in a park across the street. With increased enrollment additional space was needed, so a part of the Pierce Farm in Brookline was purchased so the boys enjoyed "the benefits of a full day in the country without unduly separating them from the influences of home life." Rivers initiated daily speeches, delivered to students gathered in the music room for non-denominational chapel services. Sometimes, he read passages from the Bible, or spoke on specific topics, such as "Why Boys Can't Get Out of Going to School." A version of Mr. Rivers' daily speeches continues to this day; students gather weekly at an all-school meeting for general announcements and special talks by members of the community. (*Courtesy of Rosalie Channing Rivers*)

Integritas et Sedulitas.

Above right: Edward Waldo Forbes (1873–1969) attended Milton Academy and graduated from Harvard. While he was at Harvard, he attended art history lectures by Charles Eliot Norton, which fostered his appreciation for art. Forbes traveled to Europe in 1908, where he studied Italian paintings and attended the University of Oxford, studying English literature. Forbes was the director of the Fogg Art Museum at Harvard University from 1909–1944. Under his leadership, the art collection was vastly expanded, and a new building was constructed in 1927. The first honorary fellowship of the International Institute for Conservation of Historic and Artistic Works was awarded to Edward Forbes in 1958.

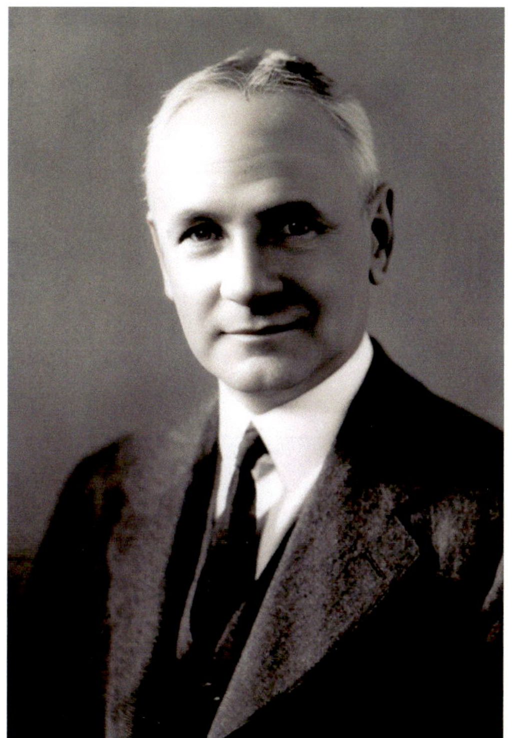 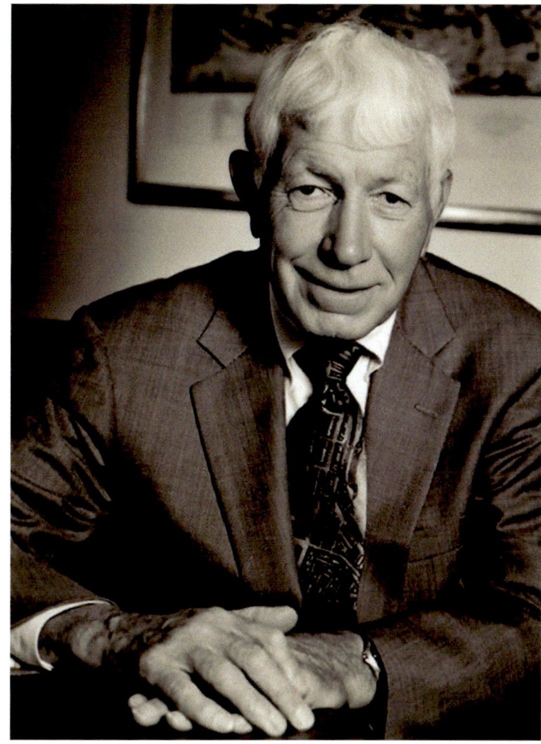

Above left: Dr. Francis Minot Rackemann (1887–1973) graduated from Harvard College and went on to graduate cum laude from Harvard Medical School. In 1914 and 1915, he worked with Warfield T. Longscope doing research on anaphylaxis. The two wrote a series of papers about allergies. Rackemann would go on to write over 175 papers on allergies. An asthma and allergy expert, he established the allergy clinic at Massachusetts General Hospital in 1919 and served as its chief from 1925–1929.

Above right: John M. Corcoran (1923–2003) graduated from Boston College after which he served in the army during World War II. He founded John M. Corcoran & Co. and Corcoran Management Co. His and his brother Leo Corcoran's leadership and high ethical standards created a culture of excellence and fair dealing at JMC, one of New England's premier real estate owners, developers, and property managers. In 2000, he donated $5 million to establish the Center for Christian-Jewish Learning at Boston College. In accordance with his wishes, the Center is committed to encouraging mutual knowledge between Christians and Jews at every level through academic research and dialogue, educational programs, and the development of resources locally, nationally, and internationally. Cororan was a trustee of Boston College and Suffolk University and served as president of the Dorchester Historical Society.

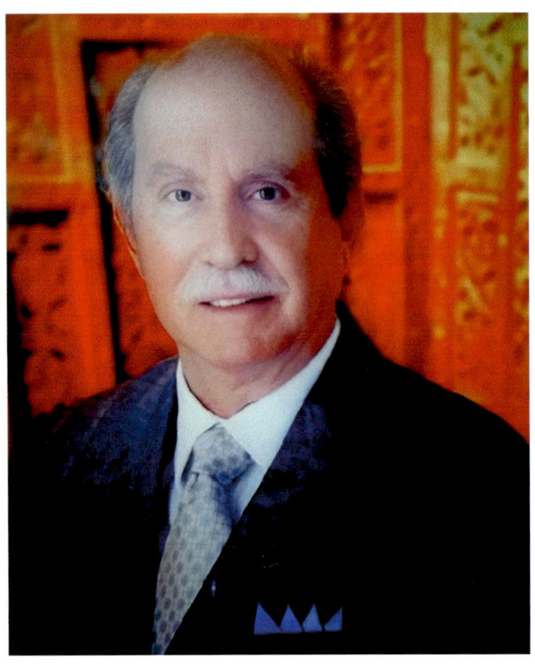

Joaquin Eduardo Bacardi, Jr. (1937–2013) attended the Fessenden School, the Dublin School, Babson College, and the University of Puerto Rico. Joaquin Bacardi started his career in Cuba as technical director of Hatuey Brewery, a predecessor to the Bacardi Corporation, based in Puerto Rico. He soon became a master blender at Bacardi, founded 1862 in Cuba by his ancestor Don Facundo Bacardi y Massó. After the 1959 Cuban Revolution, Bacardi and other family members were forced to leave Cuba and he moved to Guaynabo, Puerto Rico. He had a passion for his family legacy of rum making and flourished as a master blender until his retirement in 1984. He also served on the Bacardi Limited Board of Directors. (*Courtesy of Joyce George Bacardi*)

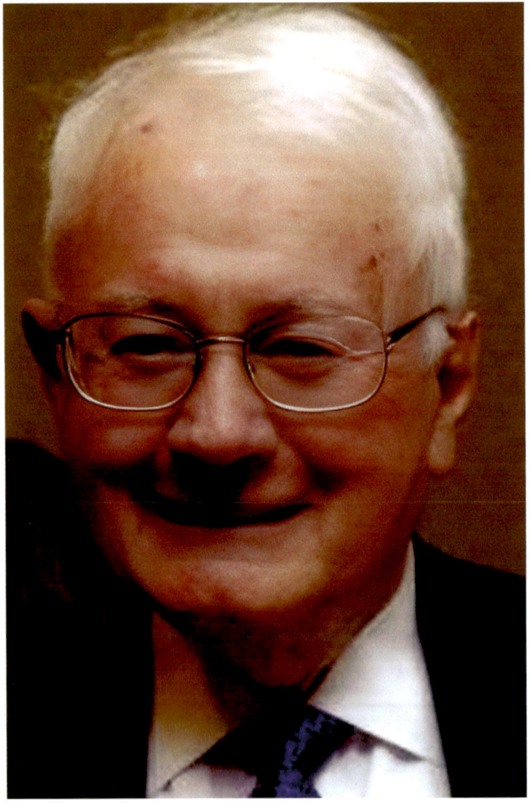

P. Leo Corcoran (1924–2010) was a partner of the John M. Corcoran & Co. and built the privately held company into a leading developer, owner, and manager of apartment communities in New England and the southeastern United States. In 1985, responding to homeless people needing safe and affordable housing, he founded Caritas Communities, Inc., a non-profit organization. His vision, leadership, and compassion to make a difference in the lives of others revitalized the concept of lodging houses with properties providing housing for men and women with low-income jobs. He and his wife, Helen Corcoran, were philanthropists, establishing the P. Leo Corcoran Foundation, and supporting Boston College, Suffolk University, Emmanuel College, Elizabeth Seton Academy, Catholic Charities, Fr. Bill's Place, St. Mary's Women's & Children, and the Sisters of Charity, Halifax.

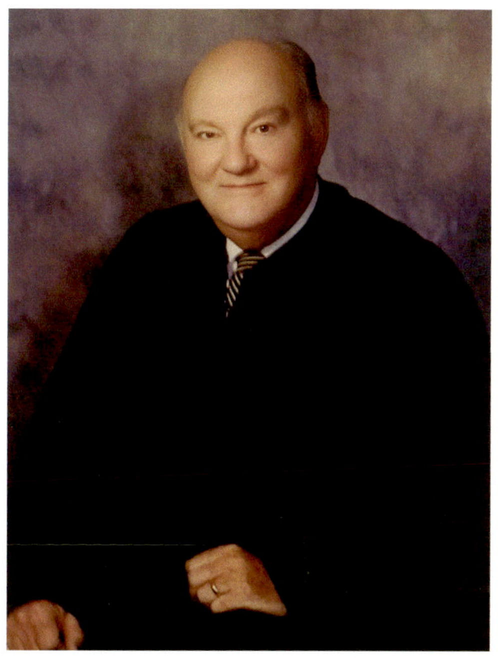

Judge John O'Brien (1930–2016) earned a Bachelor of Science degree from Boston College and was a proud 1958 graduate of New England School of Law when it was known as Portia Law School. While at Boston College, he was a reserve member of the United States Marine Corps. He was called to active duty and served in Korea from September 1950 to January 1952. He then worked at the Boston law firm of Hale, Sanderson, Byrnes & Morton. Judge O'Brien met his future law partner, John J. C. Herlihy at Hales Sanderson, and in 1975, they formed the Law Offices of Herlihy & O'Brien. On November 8, 1990, John J. O'Brien was sworn in as an associate justice of the Superior Court. He was a fellow of the American College of Trial Lawyers both as an attorney and as a judge.

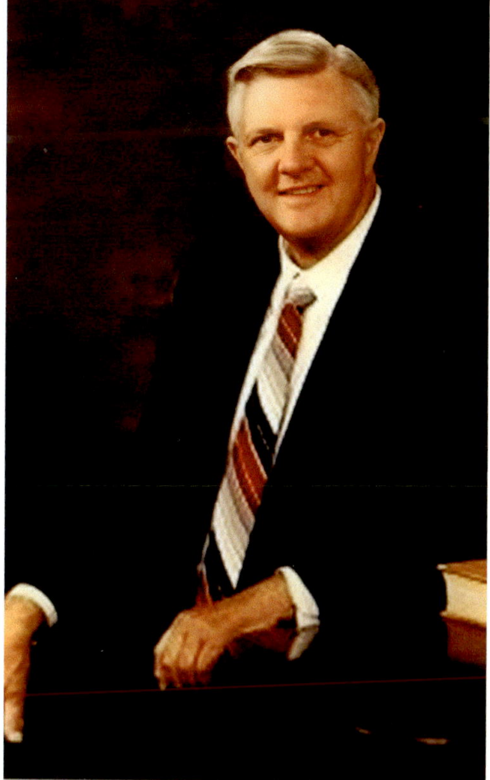

Paul V. Lyons (1939–2019) was a graduate of Boston College High School and Boston College. He earned his MBA from New York University before attending Suffolk University Law School. After earning his law degree, he worked for five years at the National Labor Relations Board. He was a partner at the law firm of Foley Hoag for over thirty years. He also served as general counsel and vice president at Suffolk University before retiring.

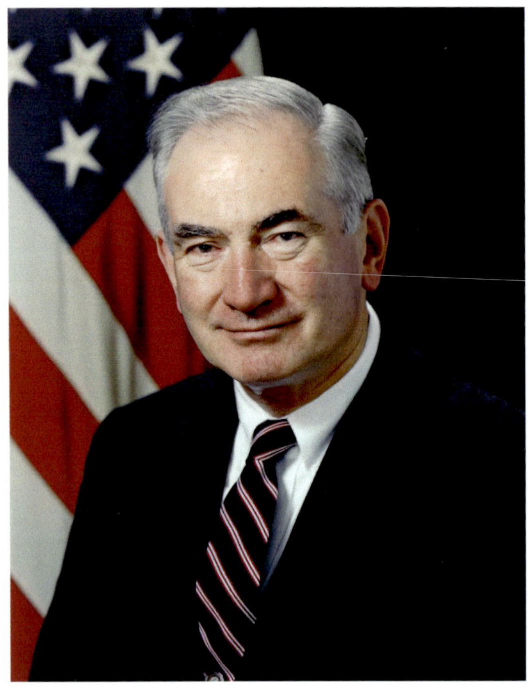

Albert J. Kelley, Jr. (1924–2004) was a graduate of Boston Latin School and received his Doctor of Science from the Massachusetts Institute of Technology. He began his career in the United States Navy as a carrier and test pilot. From 1945–1947, he served as a member of the Halsey Carrier Task Force during the Occupation of Japan, Atlantic Fleet. Kelley flew Douglas AD-4N Skyraider attack planes off carriers in the Korean Theater, worked on designing high-performance aircraft and advanced weapons, and became one of NASA's top engineering project leaders. He was senior vice president for both Arthur D. Little, Cambridge, and United Technologies and later was dean of Boston College School of Management. He served as an economic adviser to Governor Francis Sargent and the White House.

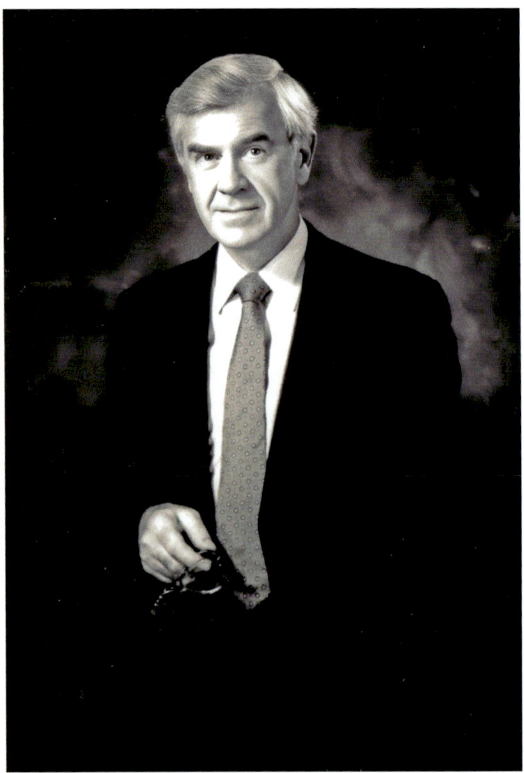

Thomas Flatley (1931–2008) was a major philanthropist and established a foundation with $200 million. Joe Corcoran said that "In real estate he was a phenomenon, really. He busted into the world of real estate and was able to do huge projects as a very young man and was doing it all his life." Flatley built office and apartment complexes, industrial parks, hotels, shopping centers, and healthcare facilities. Near the South Shore Plaza in Braintree, he built the Sheraton Tara Hotel, one of several he developed with a motif that evoked the castles of his Irish homeland. Flatley gave millions to Catholic Charities, Boston College, St. Anselm College, the New England Shelter for Homeless Veterans, and Irish causes. The *Boston Irish Famine Memorial*, sculpted by Robert Shure, was his gift in 1998 to the city of Boston.

6

MILTON ARTISTS

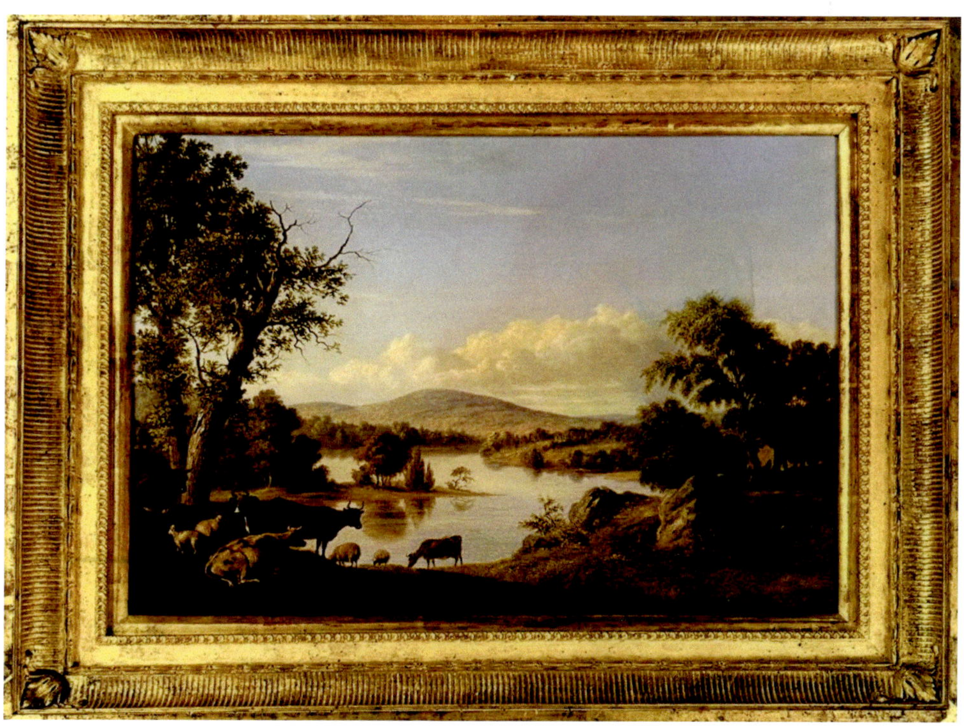

Thomas Hewes Hinckley (1813–1896) was a nineteenth-century artist who captured the bucolic and rural countryside of Milton in his oil paintings. Hinckley painted *Blue Hills from the Dedham Side* in 1848 depicting cows watering and grazing along the Neponset River. Marjorie Shaw said in her booklet *Thomas Hewes Hickley: Artist to a Generation* that "Hinckley's representation of wild and domesticated animals with their tranquil landscape settings are masterpieces of composition, brushwork, coloration and texture." (*Collection of Anthony M. Sammarco*)

79

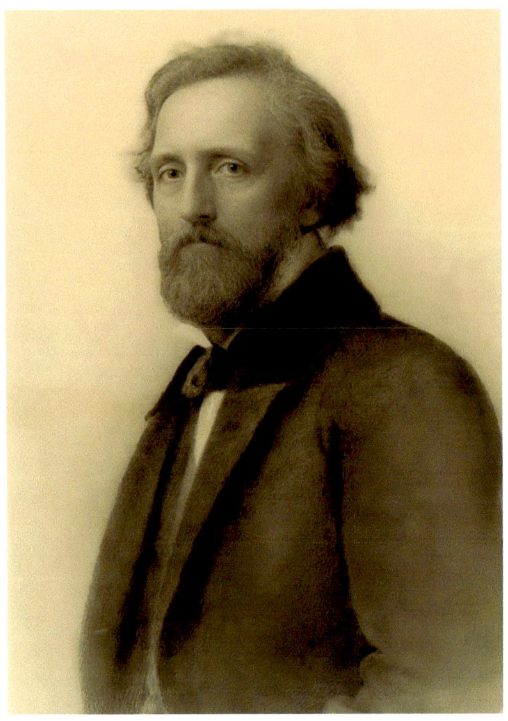

George Hollingsworth (1813–1882) attended Milton Academy and then traveled to Italy where he began formal training as a painter in Florence. While studying and copying the old masters, he also painted this self-portrait, of which he said he "was a good deal bothered in getting the drawing to look correct when reversed in the mirror." He was adept at art and skillful at teaching and became master of the Lowell Institute Drawing School at the Marlboro Chapel in Boston from 1851 until it closed in 1879. Albert Teele said of him in the *History of Milton* that he had "keen powers and habits of observation, subordinate to the discipline of his profession, imparted a clear intellectual vision and imbued his utterances even in social converse with the charm of originality." (*Collection of Museum of Fine Arts*)

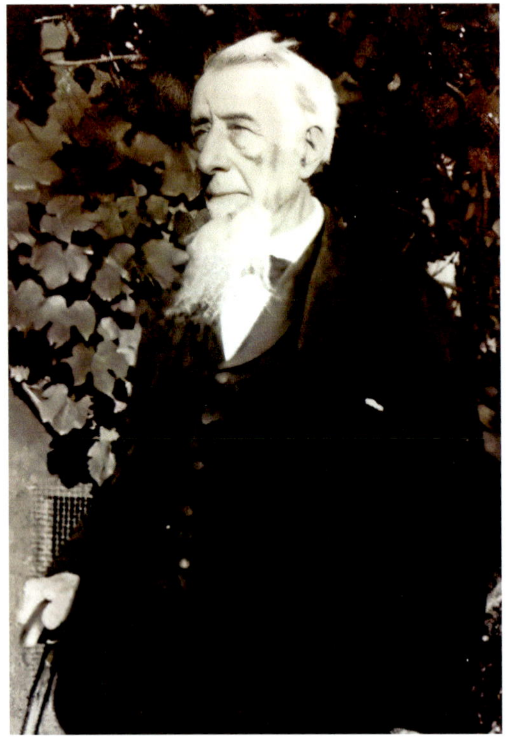

Thomas Hewes Hinckley (1813–1896) was a popular nineteenth-century painter whose early portraits memorialized his fellow Miltonians but his animal and landscape paintings depicted not just Milton, but the Adirondacks, the Catskill Mountains, and rural New England. The MET, which has his *Sketchbook of Landscape and Animal Subjects*, said that "Hinckley painted landscapes chiefly as a background to his portraits of wild and domesticated animals." In 1896, the *Milton News* said that "Hinckley never copied or imitated any other artist, believing nature to be the only true source of knowledge."

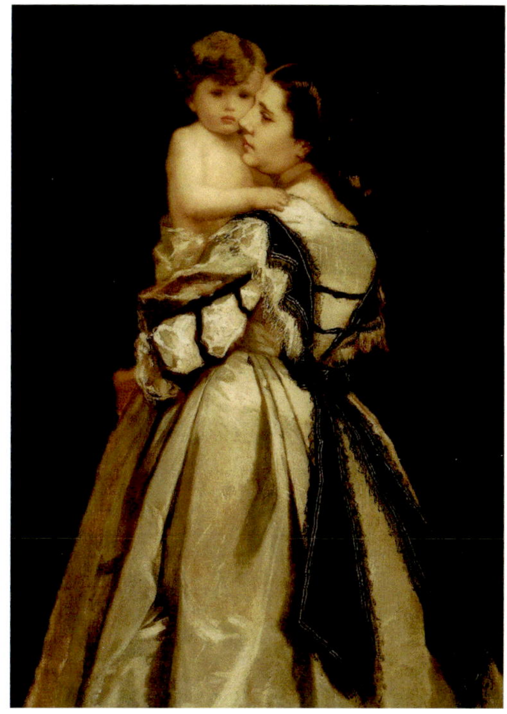

William Morris Hunt (1824–1879) painted *Mother and Child*, which depicts his wife, Louisa Dumaresq Perkins Hunt (1831–1897), and his son, Morris Hunt (1855–1858). Trained in Paris by Jean-François Millet, Hunt was to become Boston's leading portrait and landscape painter, also working as a lithographer and sculptor. In 1871, he was elected to the National Academy of Design as an associate academician. Although Hunt is buried in Brattleboro, Vermont, his family and descendants are buried at the Hunt Lot at Milton Cemetery. (*Collection of Museum of Fine Arts Boston*)

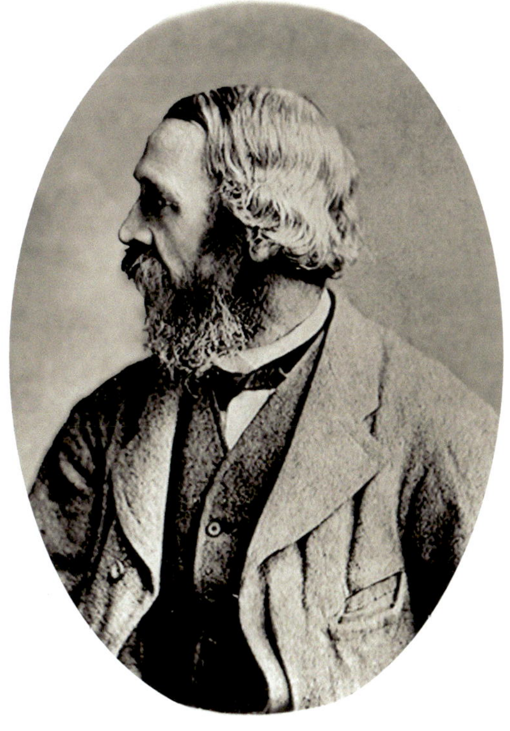

Dr. William Rimmer (1816–1879) was a sign-painter and worked as a lithographer as a young man; he went on to study with a respected physician and practiced medicine from about 1848 to about 1860. After he moved to East Milton, he began carving granite discarded from the granite dressing sheds. Through the intervention of a friend, Rimmer exhibited a plaster copy of the *Falling Gladiator* in 1863 in the Salon des Refusés in Paris, France, where it impressed visitors with its unusually realistic anatomy. Using his medical knowledge of the body, he wrote *Elements of Design* and *Art Anatomy* as well as taught at the school of the Museum of Fine Arts, Boston. A well-rounded artist, he "considered color, which he believed could by itself express the underlying meaning of an image, to be independent of form … [it] could envelope his image and assist in expressing the sentiment of the subject."

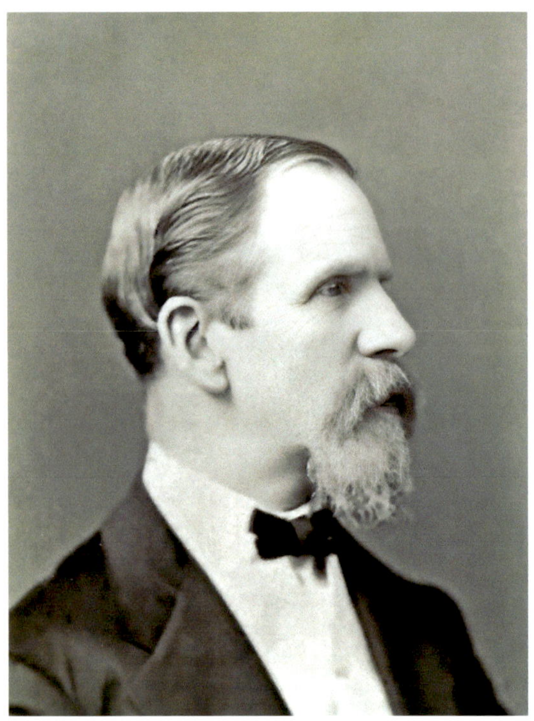

C. H. Hammatt Billings (1818–1874) was a noted architect and illustrator who designed a masthead for William Lloyd Garrison's Boston-based abolitionist newspaper, *The Liberator*, allegedly free of charge as he also was an abolitionist. He revamped the previous design by David Claypool Johnston: a slave auction on the left, and a scene of emancipation on the right, adding a central circle in which Christ stands triumphant between a kneeling slave and a fleeing slaveholder. For Harriet Beecher Stowe's book *Uncle Tom's Cabin*, Billings sketched antislavery iconography and established conventions of fine art paintings. *The Monument to the Pilgrim Forefathers* in Plymouth was designed by Hammatt Billings and begun in 1859 and was possibly his best-known design. (*Author's collection*)

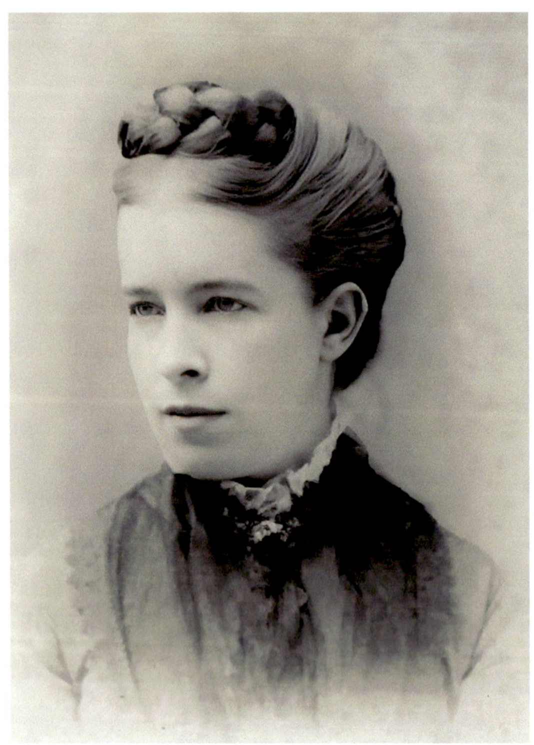

Mary Hewes Hinckley (1845–1944) attended Milton Academy Girl's School and was to become a well-regarded artist. In the *Proceedings of the Boston Natural History Museum*, Volume XI, her article "On Some Differences in the Mouth Structure of Tadpoles of the Anourous Batrachians found in Milton, Mass" thoroughly explained the many differences of tadpole's mouths and included several detailed drawings she did of them. She was also a local historian and in 1908 wrote *Sketches of Early Milton* and was co-author with Ellen Frances Vose of *Robert Vose and His Times*.

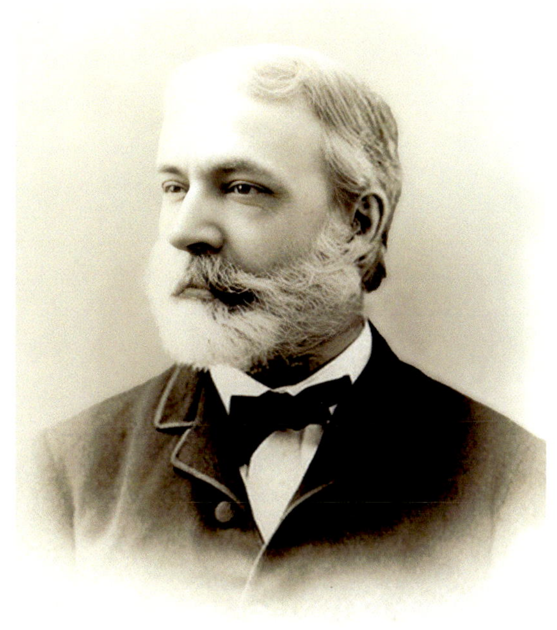

William Rotch Ware (1848–1917) graduated from Harvard and subsequently took courses in architecture at MIT before traveling to Paris to study at the École des Beaux-Arts. He was the publisher and editor of *The American Architect*, which was to become the most respected architecture periodical in North America and is today an important chronicle of late nineteenth- and early twentieth-century architecture. In his publications, Ware included clear, detailed drawings, many drawn by himself, and was an early adopter and proponent of photographic reproductions, making architectural journalism more widely accessible to architects and historians. (*Courtesy of MIT*)

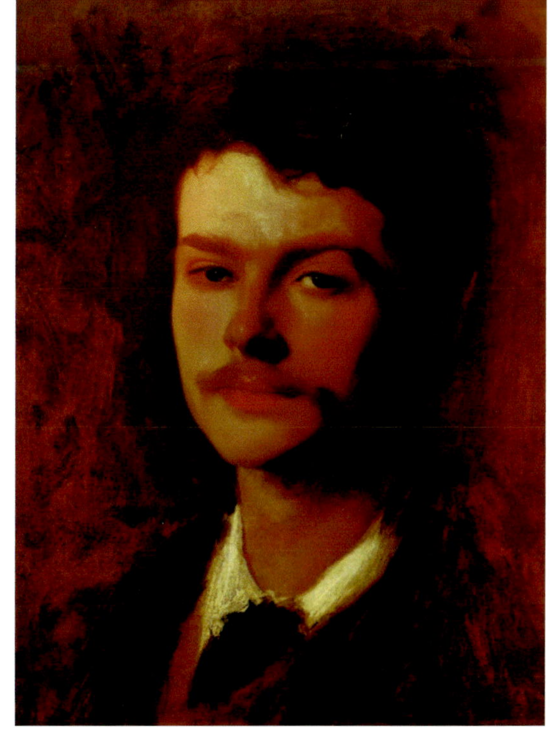

Dennis Miller Bunker (1861–1890) was a noted painter who studied at the École Nationale Supérieure des Beaux-Arts in Paris, most notably with Jean-Léon Gérôme. In 1885, Bunker was elected to the Society of American Artists and taught at the Cowles Art School. Erica Hershler of the Museum of Fine Arts said that "depending upon the viewpoint of the writer, Bunker can be seen of them as either a traditionalist or an innovator. In truth, he was both." A promising artist, he died young, and his white marble tombstone was designed by his friends Stanford White and Augustus Saint-Gaudens. (*Collection of the Tavern Club*)

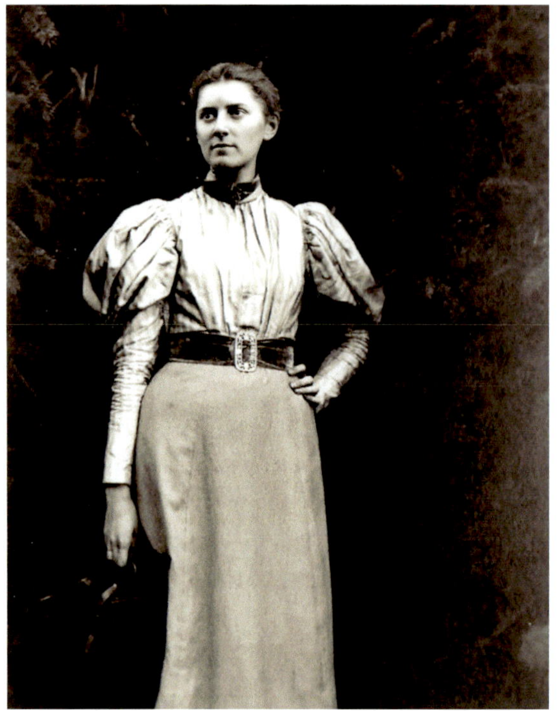

Margaret Sutermeister (1875–1950) started photography using a glass plate camera to document everyday life in Milton and the surrounding area in the late nineteenth century. Over the years, she photographed a wide range of subjects from romantic landscapes, lively street scenes, scientific experiments, and portraits both formal and candid. Among the people she photographed are Miltonians, African Americans, Gypsy vendors, farmhands at her family's nursery, and Asian laundrymen in East Milton. Her skill was evident as ten of Sutermeister's photographs are in the collection of the National Portrait Gallery. When her father died in 1909, she took over the management the family's Davenport Nursery on Canton Avenue in Milton and unfortunately gave up her penchant for photography.

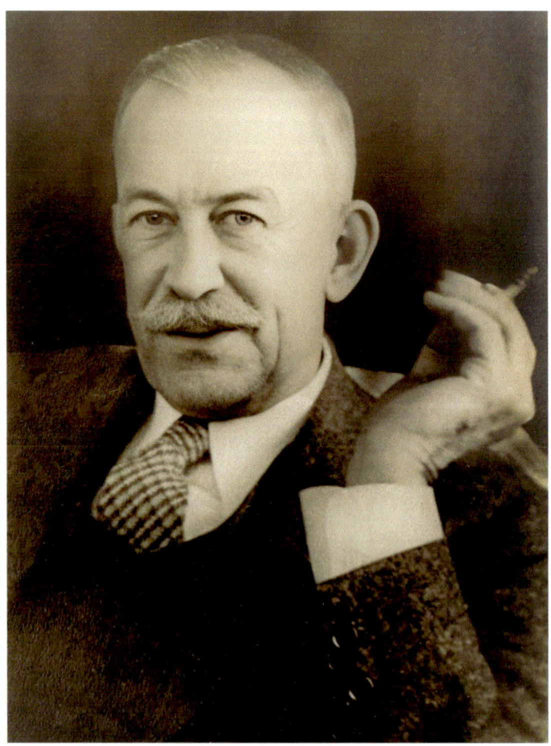

Joseph Daniels Leland (1885–1968) graduated from Harvard and studied at the Ecole des Beaux-Arts in Paris. Between 1913 and 1919, he partnered with Charles Greely Loring as Loring and Leland. After World War II, he was senior partner with Danish-born architect Niels H. Larsen in the firm of Leland and Larsen of Boston and designed Milton Hospital, the Cunningham and Collicott Schools in Milton, and the Baker Chocolate Administration Building. He served as New England director of the American Institute of Architects. However, he was also a noted watercolor artist whose nom de plume was Jose Danell. It was said that "the artist's work suggests his profession of architecture in the recurrence of a building as the central object, and in an evident comprehension of the principles of mechanics. The perspective, too, always satisfying, might further suggest this." (*Courtesy of Lysa Leland*)

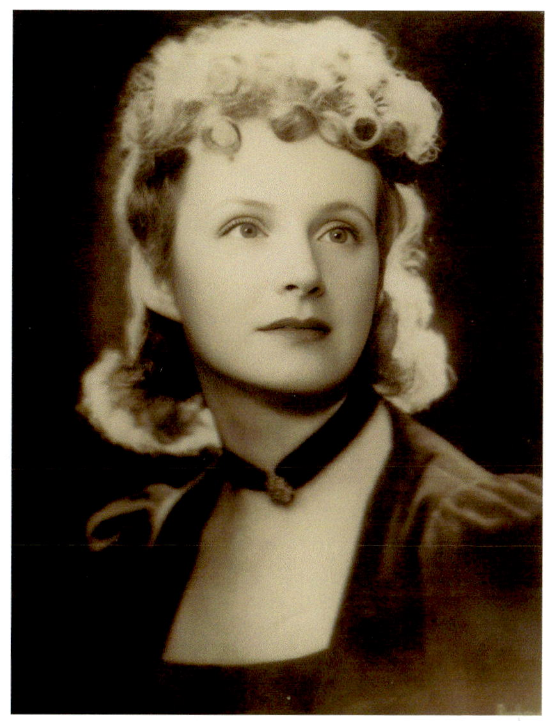

Rosamond Pier Hunt (1916–1999) was said to be one of the most respected and revered painters of the last generation, winning the most prestigious prizes in New England for her inspired watercolors. Her paintings reflected the trends of the mid-twentieth century and were exhibited widely and have a decidedly modern, somewhat cubist feeling, but are also colorful and dramatic to the extreme. With her husband, William Morris Hunt II, she is credited with founding the Cambridge Arts Festival and the Metropolitan Arts Center. (*Courtesy of Charlotte Dumaresq Hunt*)

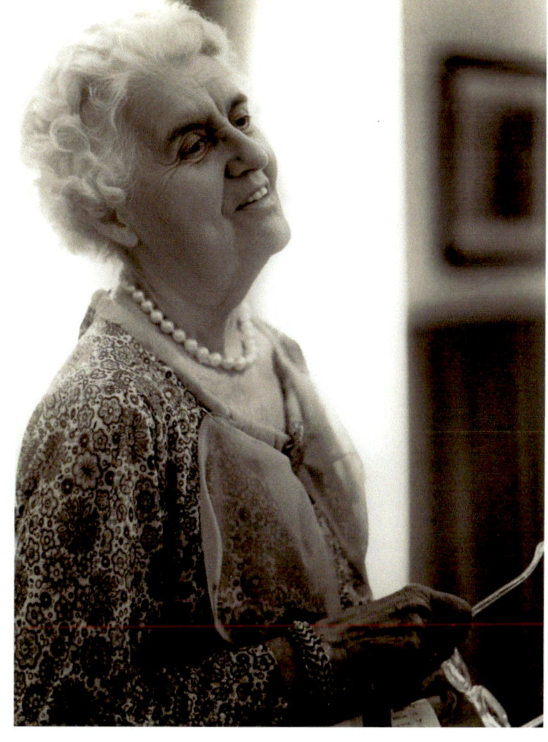

Aimée Lamb was educated at the Winsor School and the School of the Museum of Fine Arts in Boston. She studied under artists Philip L. Hale and William James. Although she is better known for her philanthropic contributions to the arts community, Miss Lamb's paintings and drawings have been represented in exhibitions with the Boston Institute of Modern Art, the Copley Society, the Boston Athenaeum, and the National Museum of Women in the Arts. She had a studio in Dublin, New Hampshire, as well as on Sutton Island, Northeast Harbor Maine. (*Author's collection*)

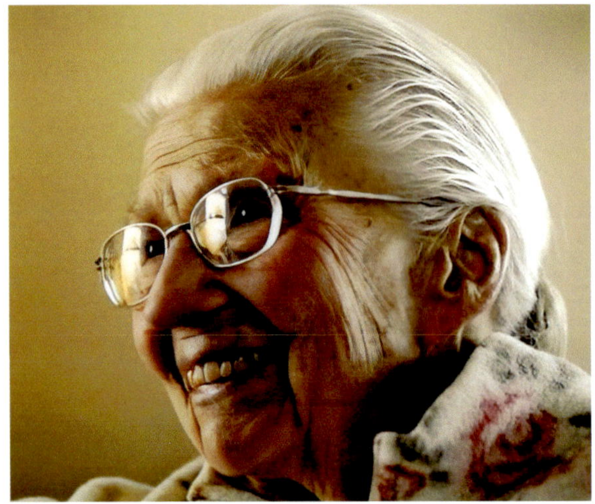

Elva Sawyer Proctor (1916–2013) attended Milton High School and the Massachusetts General Hospital School of Nursing. Well respected, her nursing career led to her becoming director of nursing services at the Boston Home in Dorchester. However, she was also a popular and talented painter and member of the Milton Art Association. Sue Sheible of the *Patriot Ledger* said that "Through her art, Elva Proctor conveys a feeling of tranquility and appreciation of life's simpler pleasures and quiet moments."

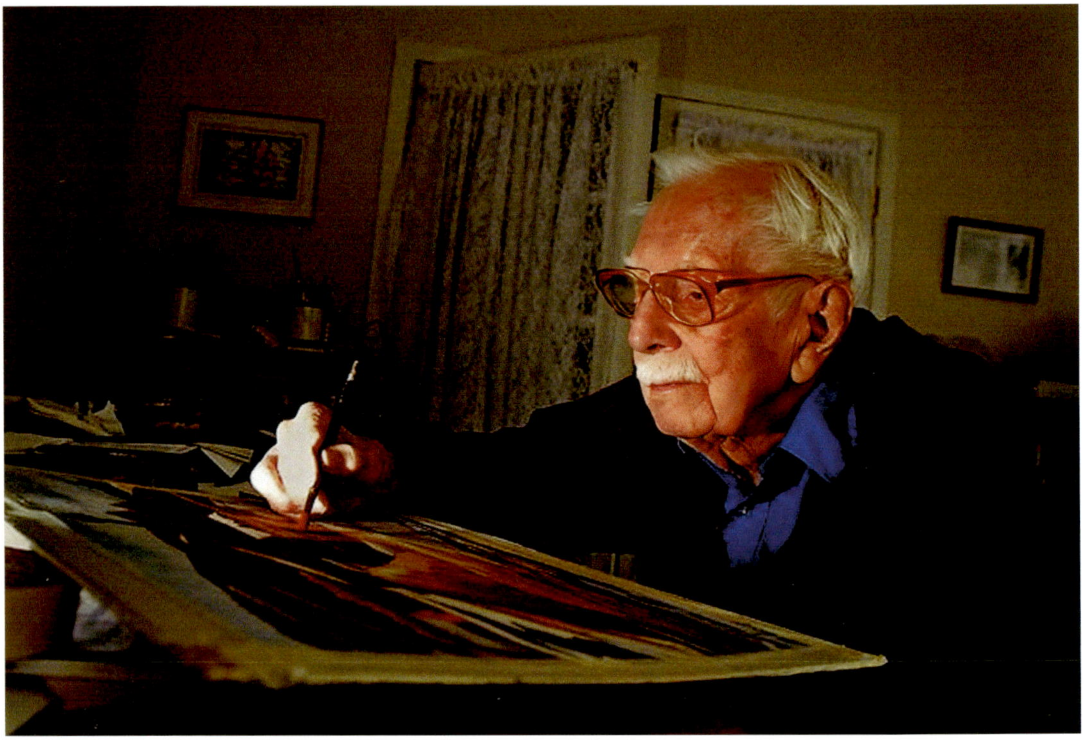

James J. Hooley, Jr. (1913–2010) was a self-taught artist whose watercolors depict such things as the Boston Public Garden, the swan boats, the Elevated Railway and Boston Street scenes. He was described as being "modest about his skills, gentle in overall demeanor and generous with the students to whom he was endeared. He pursued his craft with a quiet and steady determination however and was a prolific visual artist because of his sustained efforts." The *Patriot Ledger* said of him "While Hooley's sharp realistic style of painting remained consistent over five decades, his work also continues to exude a sense of calm, much like the artist himself."

7

MILTON AUTHORS

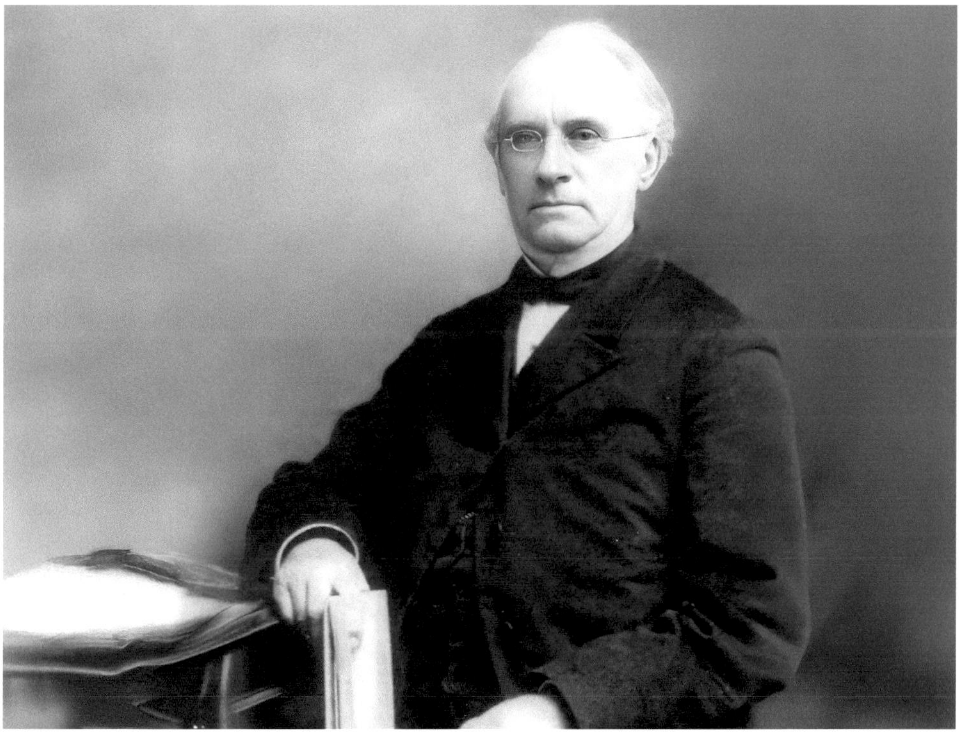

Rev. Albert Kendall Teele (1823–1901) was the minister of the First Evangelical Congregational Society in Milton from 1850–1875. A well respected Miltonian, he served as chairman of the Milton Public Library, chairman of the Milton Cemetery and chairman of the Milton School Committee. Along with J. Murray Robbins, Charles Breck, and Edmund J. Baker, he wrote and edited *The History of Milton, Mass. 1640 to 1887*, which begins stating that "God sifted a whole nation that He might send choice grain over into the wilderness." His book on the history of Milton provides tremendously important details of the town.

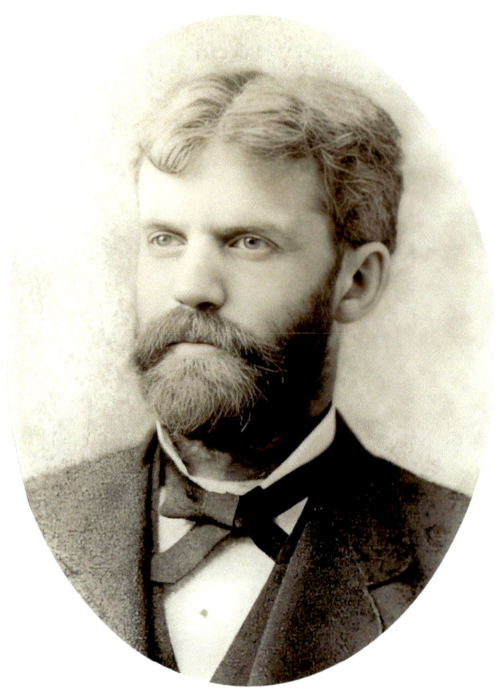

Horace Everett Ware (1845–1919) graduated from Harvard and was admitted to the Bar in 1869. He served as a member of the Massachusetts House of Representatives in 1879 and 1880. *The Farmer's Almanac* was edited by Robert Bailey Thomas, the publication's founder in 1792, becoming the *Old Farmer's Almanac* in the 1830s. Robert Ware took over as the almanac's sixth editor in 1877 and served for twenty-three years before his brother, Horace Ware, was named to the position in 1900. During Horace Everett Ware's two decades as editor, he began to shift the emphasis of the book toward a more general audience by replacing the scientific agricultural articles with general features on nature and modern life as publisher of the *Old Farmer's Almanac*. Ware was also a noted writer, among his books were *Was the Government of the Massachusetts Bay Colony a Theocracy?* and *An Incident in Winthrop's Voyage to New England*. (*Author's collection*)

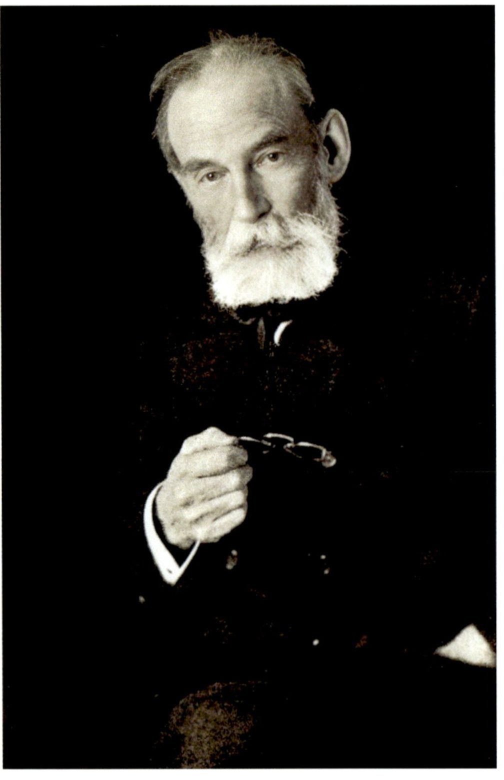

William Henry Rand (1828–1915) was an adventurer, travelling to California during the Gold Rush of the mid-nineteenth century. He later opened a printing company in Chicago and was the co-founder in 1868 with Andrew McNally, his former foreman, of the Rand McNally Publishing Company. Today, the company is one of the biggest and best-known map publishers in the United States. The company continued to grow and with the ascendancy of the automobile began a highway guide that was published annually as the *Rand McNally Official Highway Guide*.

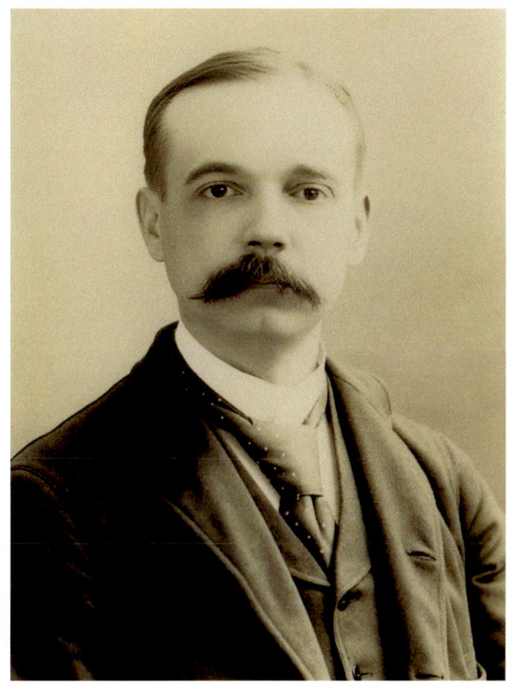

George Robert Russell Rivers (1853–1900) was an attorney and a member of the Massachusetts House of Representatives in 1892. He was a popular historical fiction author and among his books are *The Count's Snuff Box, Captain Shays: A Populist Of 1786* and *The Governor's Garden,* which was a fictional book based on history of the life of his excellency Thomas Hutchinson, sometime captain-general and governor-in-chief of his majesty's Province of Massachusetts Bay. His family lived at *Unquety,* the former home of Thomas Hutchinson on Milton Hill.

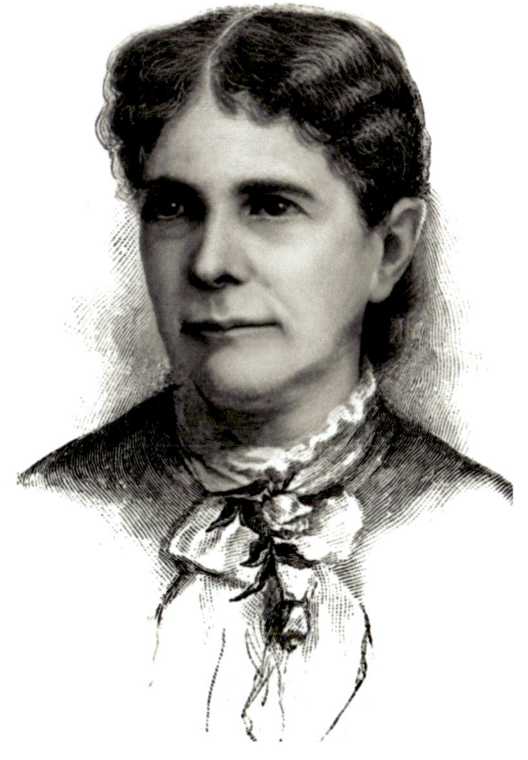

Adeline Dutton Train Whitney (1824–1906) was an American poet and prolific writer, who published more than twenty books for young girls. Her books expressed a traditional view of women's roles and were immensely popular throughout her lifetime. Whitney wrote for young girls that supported and promoted conservative values. She conveyed the message of the era that "a woman's happiest place is in the home, the source of all goodness." As this belief was popular among parents, her books sold extremely well throughout her life. *Mother Goose for Grown Folks* was written in 1859 by Whitney and illustrated by Charles Howland Hammatt Billings. For forty years she delighted her readers with *The Gayworthys, Homespun Yarns,* and *The Open Mystery: A Reading of the Mosaic Story.*

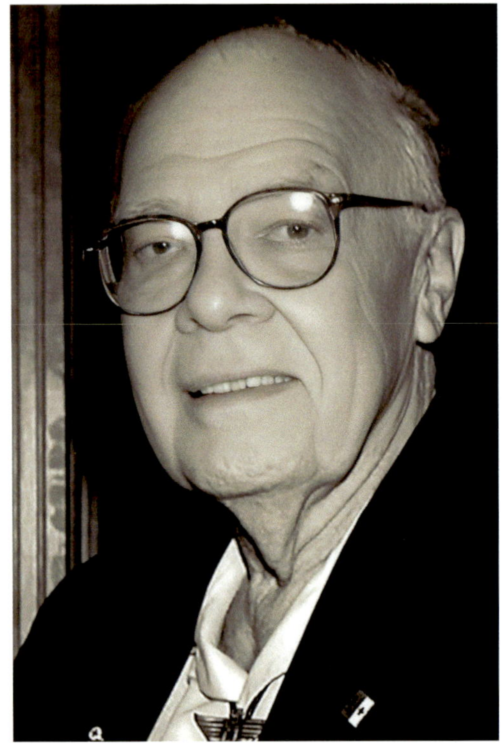

Harry Clement Stubbs (1922–2003) attended Harvard and earned an M.Ed. from Boston University and an M.S. in chemistry from Simmons College. He taught chemistry and astronomy for many years at Milton Academy. He is better known by the penname Hal Clement and was an American science fiction writer and a leader of the hard science fiction subgenre. In 1998, Clement was inducted into the Science Fiction and Fantasy Hall of Fame and was a proud member of First Fandom. He was named a grand master by the Science Fiction Writers of America in 1998 and became a Writer of Fiction judge in 2001. Clement's meticulously crafted tales of alien visitors, life-saving mathematical equations, and man-made "pseudo life" earned him the title dean of Boston Science Fiction Writers.

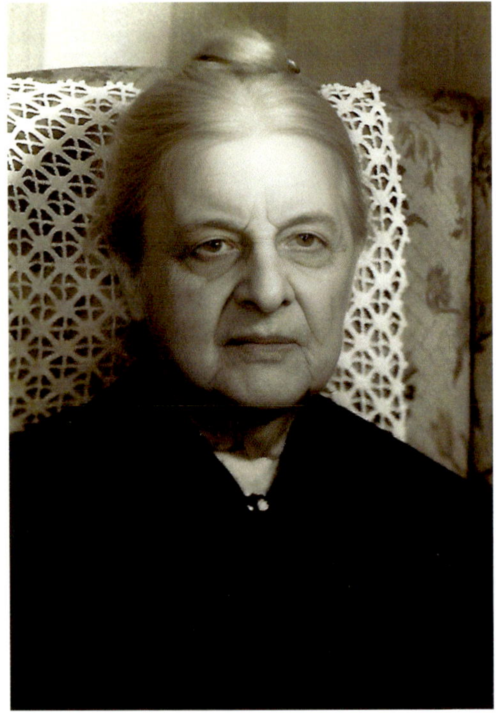

Mary Phillips Webster (1858–1950) was founder and first president of the Milton Woman's Club. A well-regarded educator, she was head of the girl's department of music at the Perkins Institution for the Blind and was a noted musical composer. Webster co-authored *The Story of the Suffolk Resolves* with Charles Morris which outlines a list of grievances drawn up in 1774 which deemed the Intolerable Acts to be unconstitutional, recognized Massachusetts as a free state, requested taxes collected from colonists to be held by the Massachusetts government, urged a boycott of goods from Britain, ended trade with Britain, and established a Massachusetts militia.

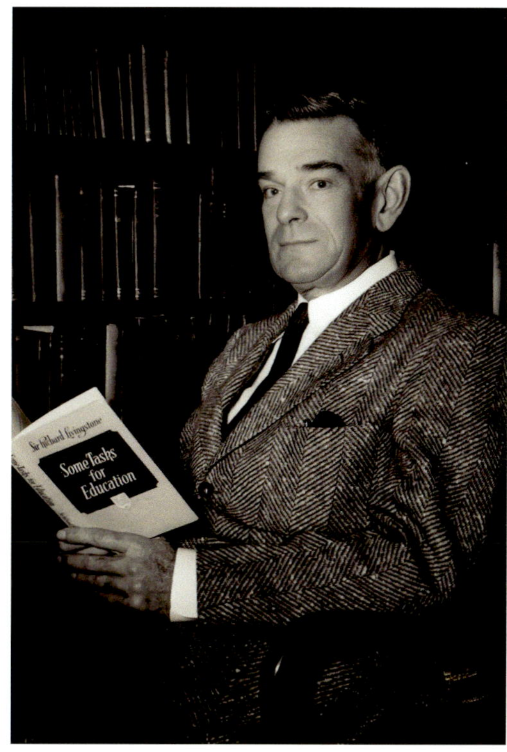

William Lusk Webster Field (1876–1963) attended Milton Academy, graduated from Harvard, and served as headmaster of Milton Academy from 1917–1942. He was a biologist, geographer, educator, academic administrator, and was elected in 1932 to the American Academy of Arts and Science. He was founder of the National Council of Independent Schools, an organization of some 700 private schools. His book *A Contribution to the Study of Individual Variation in the Wings of Lepidoptera* was highly praised. (*Courtesy of Milton Academy Archives*)

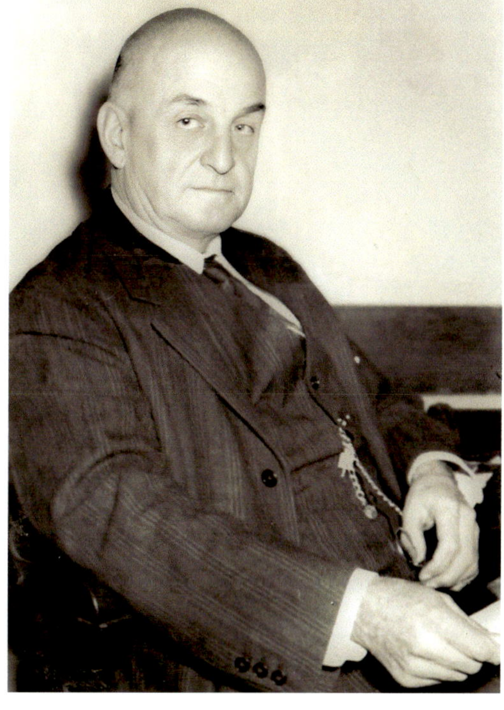

William Cameron Forbes (1870–1959) graduated from Harvard where he also served as head coach for the "Varsity Eleven" under Captain Cabot and Captain Dibblee. He was associated with the Boston engineering firm of Stone & Webster, engaged in the management of electrical properties throughout the United States. He was a partner of Forbes & Company, a family concern, and a trustee of the Baker Chocolate Company. Appointed governor general of the Philippines in 1908, he served with great éclat for five years. The people of the Philippines, primarily Tagalogs and Cebuanos, affectionately called him "Caminero" Forbes, as one resident said, "because he was responsible for the beginning of our wonderful road system here in the Philippines." In addition to good roads, he worked for good railroads, good harbors, and a sound economy. He was the author of *As to Polo*, one of his sports of choice in which he excelled.

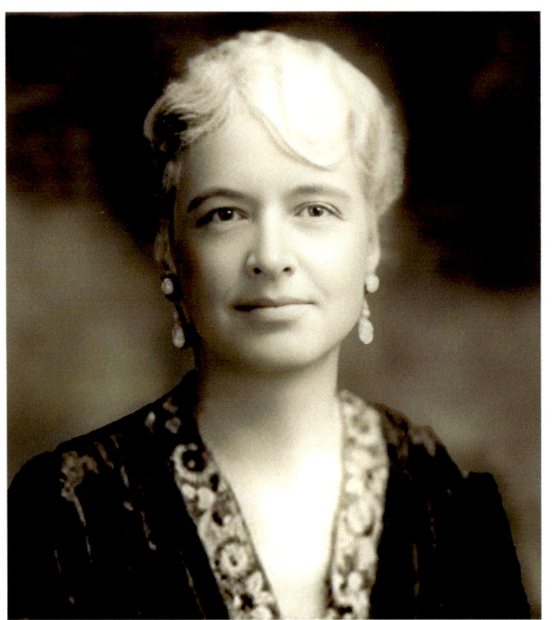 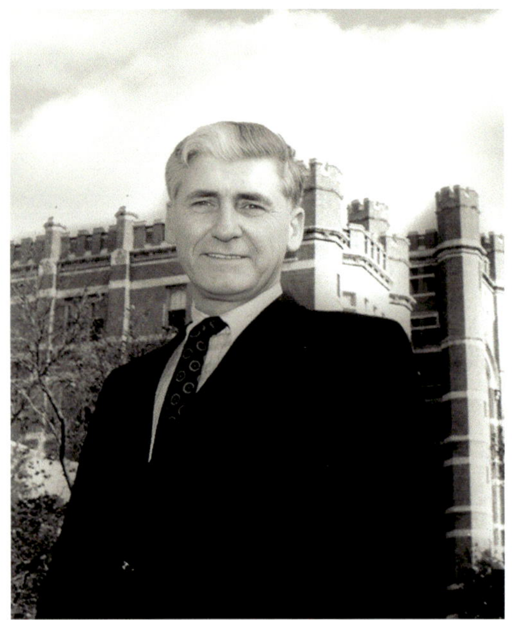

Above left: Theodora Kimball Hubbard (1887–1935) was a landscape architecture expert, librarian, editor, and author. Simmons College granted her an M.S. degree in 1917. From 1911–1924, she was librarian in the School of Landscape Architecture of Harvard University and served as special advisor there from 1924 until her death. She had worked at the School of City Planning of Harvard, as research editor, since 1929 and was an associate editor of *Landscape Architecture*, and consulting librarian and chief of the Reference Library of the United States Bureau of Industrial Housing and Transportation in Washington from 1918–1919. One of her most important works was *Municipal Accomplishment in City Planning*, a bibliography of all the works on urbanism in the United States. With her husband, Henry V. Hubbard, she wrote *An Introduction to the Study of Landscape Design.* (*Author's collection*)

Above right: Paul G. Buchanan (1927–2000) graduated from Suffolk University and was awarded a doctoral degree from Boston University. He was former assistant president of Bryant College, vice president of D'Youville College, president of Dunbarton College of the Holy Cross, and president of Annhurst College. He served as education auditor, Massachusetts State Auditor's Office, president of Milton Historical Society, and the Dorchester Historical Society and served on the Board of Trustees of Milton Public Library. He had a television program, *Our Town*, on Milton Cable Access. He was the co-author, with Anthony M. Sammarco, of *Milton: Images of America* and *Milton Architecture.* (*Courtesy of Eileen Buchanan Moncreif*)

8

S P O R T I N G *M* I L T O N

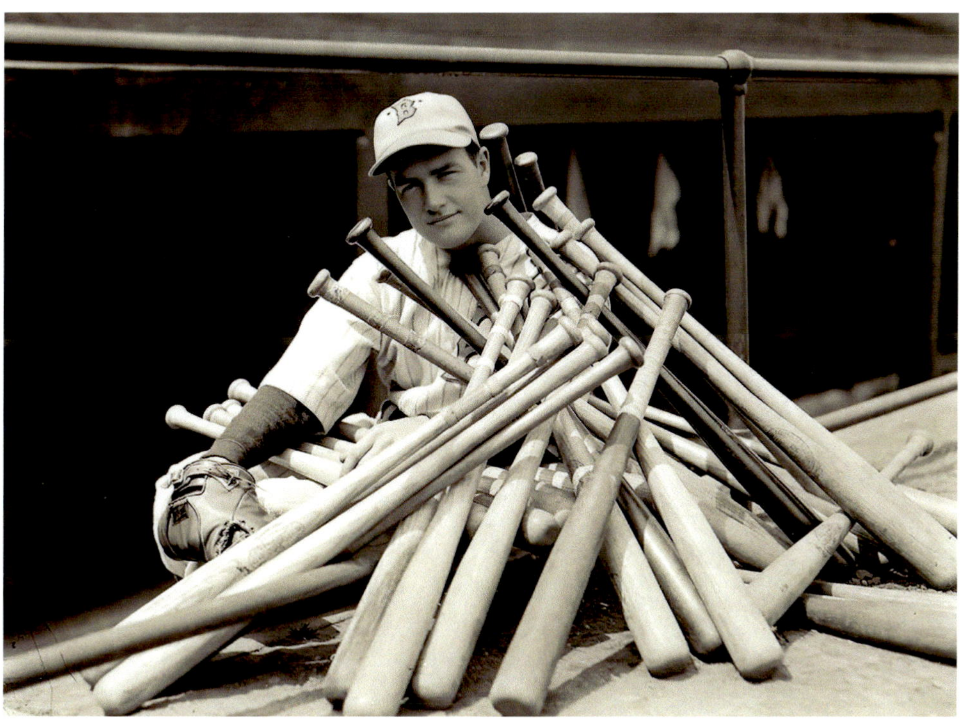

Elburt Preston Fletcher (1916–1994) attended Milton High School where he was captain of the baseball team. He is seen posing in front of the Boston Red Sox dugout with an abundance of bats. He made his major league debut in 1934 in a contest that was held to determine which Boston-area high school player was most likely to reach the major leagues, with the winner receiving an invitation to the Braves' spring training camp. Triumphant, Elbie Fletcher played with the Boston Braves (1934–35) and Boston Bees (1937–39), Pittsburgh Pirates (1939–43 and 1946–47), and Braves again (1949). During a twelve-season career, Fletcher posted a .271 batting average with 79 home runs and 616 RBI in 1,415 games played.

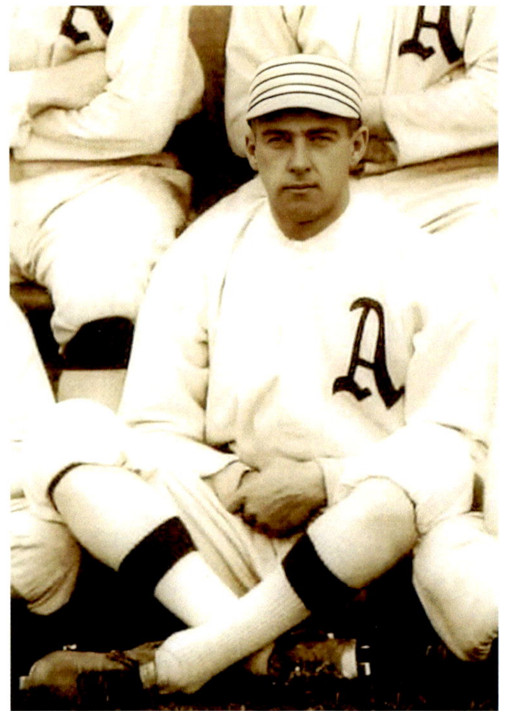

Harold Winthrop Martin (1887–1935) was attending Tufts University in 1911 when he joined the Philadelphia Athletics, a name taken from the Athletic Base Ball Club of Philadelphia, which had been a founding member of the National League in 1876. After playing baseball, he returned to college after the end of the World Series, which the Philadelphia Athletics won, although Martin did not pitch in the series. Doc Martin, as he was known as he was studying to become a doctor, played for the Philadelphia Athletics during the 1911 and 1912 seasons but only pitched in two games for the Athletics in 1912 and never played professionally again.

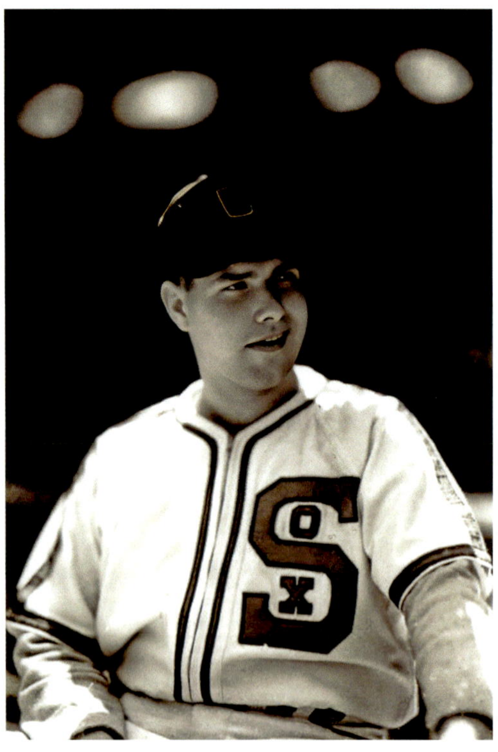

William Vincent Chamberlain (1909–1994) attended Dean Academy and Saint Anselm College where he was on the baseball team. Chamberlain was pitching for Harwich in the Cape Cod Baseball League in 1932 when he was noticed by a Chicago White Sox scout, and he was playing in Chicago by the end of the season. He played twelve games for the Chicago White Sox, starting five and losing all of them. But even though Chamberlain never won a big-league game, he played in the minors until the end of the 1938 season, making stops in the International, Texas, Eastern, New York-Pennsylvania, Northeastern, and Cape Breton Colliery leagues. After baseball, he served as a Boston policeman.

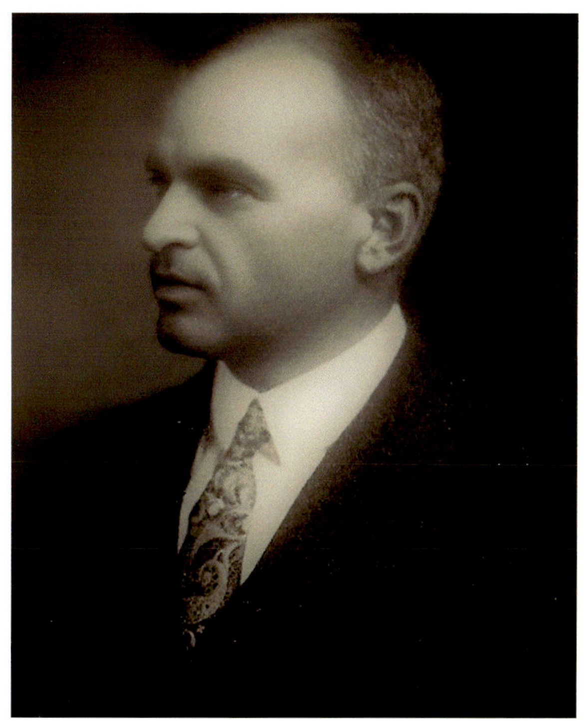

Charles Morgan Rotch (1878–1964) was the president of the Boston Skating Club for twenty-five years, and thereafter served as chairman of the Board of Governors until his death. Rotch was always progressive in outlook, skillful in the handling of intricate problems, diplomatic in his dealings with others and always kindly and considerate to everyone with whom he came in contact. Under his leadership and during his presidency, all the dreams of the earlier years, including the building of the club's own rink in Allston, were fulfilled. He also played a leading role in the promotion of international participation in the sport of skating, as well as in guiding the activities of the U.S. Figure Skating Club, twice as its president and as a long-time World and Olympic Championship referee and judge. (*Courtesy of Boston Skating Club*)

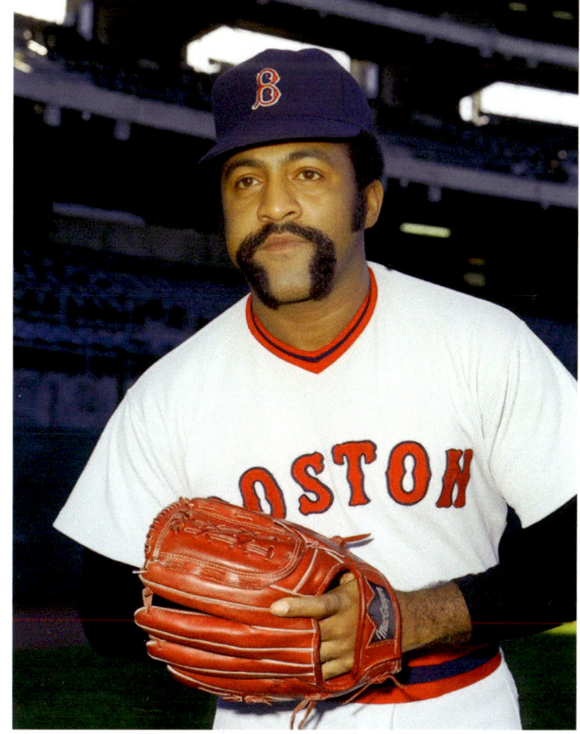

Luis Clemente Tiant Vega (1940–2024) was a second-generation baseball player. His father Luis Eleuterrio Tiant (1906–1976) was considered the finest baseball pitcher from Cuba playing in the Cuba Club. He played for the Havana Red Sox, Cuban Stars West, Cuban House of David, Pollock's Cuban Stars, and New York Cubans, between 1928 and 1947. His son was Luis Clemente Tiant Vega, nicknamed El Tiante, a member of the Boston Red Sox. Tiant was inducted to the Boston Red Sox Hall of Fame in 1997, the Hispanic Heritage Baseball Museum Hall of Fame in 2002, the Venezuelan Baseball Hall of Fame and Museum in 2009, and the Baseball Reliquary's Shrine of the Eternals in 2012.

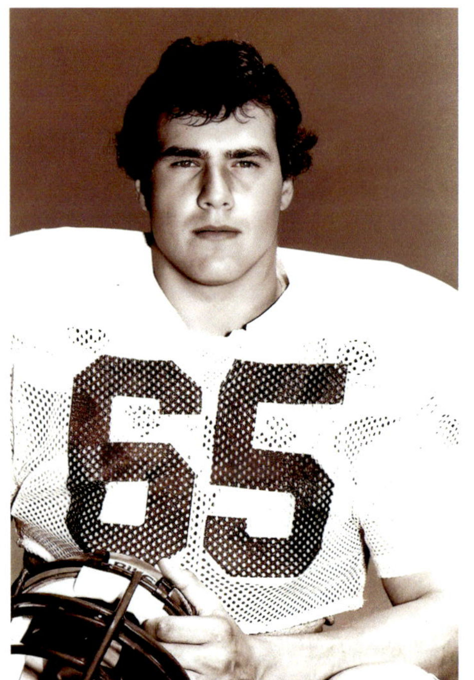

Steve Trapilo (1964–2004) attended Boston College High School and Boston College where he played offensive guard for the Eagles from 1982–1986. He was drafted in the fourth round of the 1987 National Football League (NFL) draft by the New Orleans Saints. He played with the New Orleans Saints from 1987–1990, and again in 1992 and was selected by the Saints in the fourth round of the 1987 NFL draft. He provided a key block for Doug Flutie in the famed "Miracle in Miami" Hail Mary pass in 1984. Trapilo was inducted into the Boston College Varsity Club Athletic Hall of Fame in 2001.

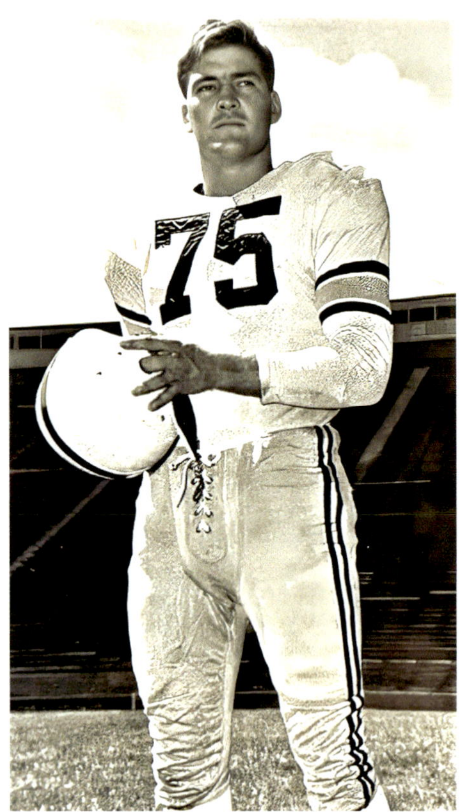

Lloyd H. Hill, Sr. (1928–2022) was a graduate of Brown University, Bridgewater State University, M. Ed and Suffolk University, JD. He was captain of the football team at Brockton High School and was captain and All-American football tackle at Brown where he was named to the Athletic Hall of Fame. He was signed with the Steelers, but he was drafted to serve in the Korean War, where he served with distinction. An avid runner, he completed thirty-seven Boston Marathons. An adjunct professor at Northeastern University and Quincy College, Hill worked as a dedicated and respected educator serving the Quincy community. Hill's career spanned thirty-five years as an administrator and coach with his final twenty years as the principal, and greatest fan, of his cherished Quincy High School Presidents where the Lloyd Hill Center for Performing Arts was named in his honor.